THE LUMINOUS DARKNESS

THE NEGRO SPIRITUAL SPEAKS
OF LIFE AND DEATH

JESUS AND THE DISINHERITED

DEEP IS THE HUNGER

MEDITATIONS OF THE HEART

THE CREATIVE ENCOUNTER

DEEP RIVER

THE GROWING EDGE

FOOTPRINTS OF A DREAM

THE INWARD JOURNEY

TEMPTATIONS OF JESUS

DISCIPLINES OF THE SPIRIT

THE LUMINOUS DARKNESS

THE LUMINOUS DARKNESS

by
Howard Thurman

A Personal Interpretation
of the Anatomy of Segregation
and the Ground of Hope

Friends United Press
Richmond, Indiana

Library of Congress Cataloging-in-Publication Data

Thurman, Howard, 1900-1981.
 The luminous darkness : a personal interpretation of the anatomy
of segregation and the ground of hope / by Howard Thurman. — 1st
pbk. ed.
     p. cm.
 Reprint. Originally published: 1st ed. New York : Harper & Row,
1965.
 ISBN 0-944350-07-0
 1. Afro-Americans—Segregation. 2. Race relations—Religious
aspects—Christianity. 3. Thurman, Howard, 1900-1981. I. Title.
E185.61.T47 1989
 305.8'96073'0924—dc19
 [B]   89-30926
                                                                    CIP

To

MOTHER BAILEY

who inspired generations of young Negroes to sense
the luminous quality of darkness

PROLOGUE

In an appendix to a term paper, one of my students included the following in his description of his experience as a deep-sea diver:

"Enroute to the floor of the ocean the diver first passes through the 'belt of the fishes.' This is a wide band of light reflected from the surface of the sea. From this area he moves to a depth of water that cannot be penetrated by light above the surface. It is dark, forboding, and eerie. The diver's immediate reaction is apt to be one of fear and sometimes a sudden spasm of panic that soon passes. As he drops deeper and deeper into the abyss, slowly his eyes begin to pick up the luminous quality of the darkness; what was fear is relaxed and he moves into the lower region with confidence and peculiar vision."

> If I say, Surely the darkness shall cover me
> Even the night shall be light about me . . .
> The darkness and the light are both alike to Thee.
>
> PSALM 139:11-12
>
> HOWARD THURMAN

FOREWORD

This is an essay. It is, as the subtitle suggests, a personal interpretation of the anatomy of segregation and a testimony as to the
grounds of hope for the individual. It is not a chronicle of the
civil rights upheaval nor is it an interpretation of the social revolu-
tion of which the struggle for civil rights is a part. No effort has
been made to assess the improvements that have taken place in
the relation between the Negro American and the white American,
nor to analyze the meaning of such developments. Quite deliberately
I have refrained from discussing the organizations that have
emerged to deal with the social crisis that is upon us and those
that have been at work in the long weary years when there were

no lights on the horizon and few voices to be heard in the land. Only incidental mention has been made of the heroes, the martyrs, and the leaders, some of whose names are household words wherever men tarry to talk seriously of the times in which we live and the goals of our strivings. The depth and extent of my support and involvement need not be reported here.

The fact that the first twenty-three years of my life were spent in Florida and in Georgia has left its scars deep in my spirit and has rendered me terribly sensitive to the churning abyss separating white from black. Living outside of the region, I am aware of the national span of racial prejudice and the virus of segregation that undermines the vitality of American life. Nevertheless, a strange necessity has been laid upon me to devote my life to the central concern that transcends the walls that divide and would achieve in literal fact what is experienced as literal truth: human life is one and all men are members one of another. And this insight is spiritual and it is the hard core of religious experience.

My roots are deep in the throbbing reality of the Negro idiom and from it I draw a full measure of inspiration and vitality. I know that a man must be at home somewhere before he can feel at home everywhere. Always the sense of separateness that is an essential part of individual consciousness must be overcome even as it sustains and supports. This is the crucial paradox in the achievement of an integrated personality as well as of an integrated society. To work as if the walls did not exist, to be nourished by the strength of one's ethnic idiom, and at the same time to be victimized by the walls is as exhilarating as it is hazardous. There is no waking moment or sleeping interval when one may expect respite from the desolation and despair of segregation.

There is no more fitting way to make an end of this Foreword than to quote a part of the final paragraph in my Ingersoll Lecture on *The Negro Spiritual Speaks of Life and Death.* "They [the slaves] made a worthless life, the life of chattel property, a mere thing, a body, *worth living.* They yielded with abiding enthusiasm to a view of life which included all the events of their experience without exhausting themselves in those experiences. To them this quality of life was insistent fact because of that which deep within them, they discovered of God, and His far-flung purposes. God was not through with them. And He was not, nor could He be exhausted by, any single experience or any series of experiences. To know Him was to live a life worthy of the loftiest meaning of life. Men in all ages and climes, slave or free, trained or untutored, who have sensed the same values, are their fellow-pilgrims who journey together with them in increasing self-realization in quest for the city that hath foundations, whose Builder and Maker is God."

●

Wherever it has seemed pertinent to use incidents or materials that have appeared in my earlier writing, I have done so.

THE LUMINOUS DARKNESS

ONE OF THE CENTRAL PROBLEMS IN HUMAN relations is applying the ethic of respect for personality in a way that is not governed by special categories. The question keeps intruding, "Does the category by which life is defined decree how the ethic shall be applied?" For instance, if a man is committed to a reverent view of life, does he rule out high regard for life that threatens or seems dangerous to him? If a particular man, by definition, is not human, then may not the ethical behavior that usually applies be suspended? Does a man tend to become immoral and irreligious as his security is threatened?

It is part of the wisdom of the Judaeo-Christian ethic that all

1

men are enjoined to love God and to love one another. However ardently a man may hold to this attitude, his commitment is nevertheless threatened by the reality that he still will admit categories of exception and extenuating circumstances which amend and sometimes nullify his respect for human life.

During World War II I lived in California. It was not infrequent that one saw billboard caricatures of the Japanese: grotesque faces, huge buck teeth, large dark-rimmed thick-lensed eyeglasses. The point was, in effect, to read the Japanese out of the human race; they were construed as monsters and as such stood in immediate candidacy for destruction. They were so defined as to be placed in a category to which ordinary decent behavior did not apply. Without any apparent wrench of conscience or violation of due process, it was possible for the entire Japanese-American community to be removed from the West Coast and placed in relocation camps in the center of the country. It was open season for their potential extermination, thus providing immunity from guilt feelings. During World War I the same behavior was directed toward the Germans and people of German descent. Many churches and ministers joined in the practice. I have a friend who was so deeply injured by her experiences of this behavior during the war that she still cannot bring herself to attend Christian religious services of any kind. So conditioned was she that during World War II she lived in muted terror which expressed itself in the kind of alarm she showed whenever her doorbell rang in the early morning or in the late evening.

This, in broad outline, indicates the moral climate in which Negroes and white persons have lived in the United States. The Christian ethic has been deeply influenced by this circumstance.

2

For a long time the Christian Church has profoundly compromised with the demands of the Gospel of Jesus Christ, especially with respect to the meaning and practice of love.

When I was a boy growing up in Florida, it never occurred to me, nor was I taught either at home or in church, to regard white persons as falling within the scope of the magnetic field of my morality. To all white persons, the category of exception applied. I did not regard them as involved in my religious reference. They were not read out of the human race—they simply did not belong to it in the first place. Behavior toward them was amoral. They were not hated particularly; they were not essentially despised; they were simply out of bounds. It is very difficult to put into words what was at work here. They were tolerated as a vital part of the environment, but they did not count *in*. They were in a world apart, in another universe of discourse. To lie to them or to deceive them had no moral relevancy; no category of guilt was involved in my behavior. There was fear of their power over my life; the meaning and the basis of this fear will be discussed at another point in my essay.

What was true for me as a boy was true also of any little white boy in my town with an important and crucial difference! The structure of the society was such that I was always at his mercy. He was guaranteed by his society; I was not. I was always available as an outlet for his hostility whatever may have been the cause of his hostility. If he was angry because he had been chastised by his parents or because of something else that had happened to him in his world and he met me on the street, he could easily give vent to his anger. He could molest me or push me off the sidewalk without too great a danger of retaliation. Or if he was just out for "kicks" he could do the same thing and most often be protected by his group. Thus I was taught to keep out of his way, to reduce my exposure to him under any and all circumstances. I lived in a segregated world into which he could come and go at will; but into his world I could go only when directed or on business. His behavior tended to be unpredictable and irresponsible, therefore in no sense binding upon him. I was frozen in my status; he was fluid in his.

Precisely what does it mean to be frozen in one's status? The issue is not one of law or legality as expressed in statutes. These are after the fact. There is something deeper at work. That it was a violation of the law of the state and the ordinances of my town for me to enter the public library as a patron or to borrow a book was not the immediately prohibiting element. It was taken for granted that the very existence of law was for the protection and the security of white society. The frozen status was a way of living; it was a part of the common life. It was to function without any collective consensus of security. Always and everywhere you were strictly on your own and your life depended upon the survival techniques you had learned in the living.

As I look back upon those days, I never gave to the way of living demanded of me by my environment, the inner sanction of my spirit. I gave to it what may be called the sanction of strategy. There was a place in me untouched by these pressures on my life. At the same time I was not consciously involved in deep inner conflict, since the sensitive area of my own ethics had not been implicated in the issues of my life of segregation. The tragedy was that no ethical judgment prevailed. Living in a frozen status established the boundaries of my moral concern. Those who were a

4

part of my segregated world came under the judgment of my interpretation of the meaning of religion. It made for a peculiar kind of self-righteousness. The common saying in my world was: the white man did not have any religion. By implication we did. That kept me from expecting him to act toward me as I would expect a fellow Christian to act, but curiously enough my religion did not demand of me that I act toward him as a Christian should act. At the risk of being repetitious, he was not regarded as worthy of a Christian response. It was a cruel dilemma; the price paid for a kind of inner balance that would make for some measure of peace of mind was the rigid narrowing or restricting of the Christian ethic. The struggle was to try to achieve a sense of self in a total environment that threatened the self.

●

It is clear that for the Negro the fundamental issue involved in the experience of segregation is the attack that it makes on his dignity and integrity. We become persons by an other-than-self reference which is other persons. We become human in a human situation. The primary group with which this process is immediately associated is the family. The sense of being deeply cared for and protected and loved in the immediate family provides the firm ground of security for the self. The mother and the father of the child, the adult, prestigious members of the family and intimates—these are the points of reference for the child.

It is difficult to assess what happens to the child in an environment where he sees his parents and other adults humiliated and reduced to insignificance by the treatment received from certain

5

white persons in the general environment. To experience their defenselessness and at the same time to regard them as his defenders is cruel and rottening to the self. Always a way has had to be found for handling this contradiction.

Segregation gives rise to an immoral exercise of power of the strong over the weak, that is to say, advantage over disadvantage. The restrictions affecting the disadvantaged, the Negroes, are mandatory, while there is a voluntary element in the way the same restrictions affect white persons. Segregation has a margin of freedom of movement without threat, always available to the powerful but not available to the weak. In the old days on the Jim Crow trains in the South, the white conductor used double seats in the Negro section of a car as his office. Often that would leave only six other seats for Negro passengers. If the seats were taken when you got on the train, you stood up to the end of your journey, regardless of the many vacant seats in the white coach. If you tried to sit in the conductor's seats, he would usually get the Negro porter to move you. Rarely would he himself become directly involved in any conversation with Negro passengers.

In American society generally, formal power rests largely within the white community. In white society is the citadel of the so-called power structure. The controls that determine the establishment and maintenance of law and order reside there. For this reason, prestigious members of the group can and often do function without social and moral responsibility. Segregation is at once one of the most blatant forms of moral irresponsibility. The segregated persons are out of bounds, are outside the magnetic field of ethical concern. It is always open season. The reason has been previously discussed. This was the general climate and the Christian ethic made no impact. Of course the radical difference between the position of Negroes and white persons as regards the effect of social irresponsibility was the difference in power. The idea that a Negro interpreted the white person as being out of bounds had a limited scope in which to operate because of the strictures under which he was forced to live. The power of the white person tended to take all integrity out of his personal relations with Negroes, but it did not affect him materially in his function in the world in which he had established controls. In short, he was less vulnerable than the Negro because he was a white man.

On the other hand, his power gave him a wide range of opportunities to affect the life of Negroes without responsibility. He could even damage his person with immunity. To illustrate how deeply involved is the issue here: When I was a boy I earned money in the fall of the year by raking leaves in the yard of a white family. I did this in the afternoon, after school. In this family there was a little girl about six or seven years old. She delighted in following me around the yard as I worked. One of her insistences was to scatter the piles of leaves in order to find a particular shape to show me. Each time it meant that I had to do my raking all over again. Despite my urging she refused to stop what she was doing. Finally I told her that I would report her to her father when he came home. This was a real threat to her because she stood in great fear of her father. She stopped, looked at me in anger, took a straight pin out of her pinafore, ran up to me and stuck me with the pin on the back of my hand. I pulled back my hand and exclaimed, "Ouch! Have you lost your mind?" Whereupon she said in utter astonishment, "That did not hurt you—you can't feel."

In other words, I was not human, nor was I even a creature capable of feeling pain. Manifestly this is an extreme position, but it indicates the social and psychological climate in which it would be possible for a little girl to grow up in a Christian family with such a spontaneous attitude toward other human beings. Segregation guarantees such inhumaneness and throws wide the door for a complete range of socially irresponsible behavior. This obtains for the segregated and the separated; for under the system white persons are separated from Negroes but they are not segregated— only the Negroes are segregated. There can be shuttling back and forth between the two worlds by the separated but not so for the segregated.

The fact that the status of the Negro in a segregated society is frozen does not mean that he is without a special kind of power. In order to keep his status frozen, many things must be done within the white society which limit its development and hamper its enrichment. When a new law for the common good is being considered, before the merits of the law itself can be examined, there is a previous consideration that must be taken into account: what bearing will the new law have on the relationship between whites and Negroes? A way must always be found that will provide maximum benefit to the white community and minimum benefit to the Negro community. The touchstone is not to disturb the fixed status while at the same time to develop increased freedom for growth and development within the white community. How much improvement can be given to the schools for white children without providing a similar improvement to the schools for Negro children? How much improvement can be made in city streets and lighting without improving streets in the Negro community? If there is a

8

county or state fair, what can be done so as to exclude Negroes or include them as insignificantly as possible? Can white society function as if Negroes did not exist, or if their existence is acknowledged, can this be done so as not to encourage their getting out of their place?

●

But any society is apt to be so viable that things are always shifting and are constantly being influenced by the larger community of the country and the world. The blame for unwelcome change can easily be ascribed to the influence or activity of the outsider. The common cry in the South is that everything was moving along quite peacefully until the agitator from the outside interfered. The notion that segregated persons would ever of themselves on their own volition want conditions to change is impossible to entertain. And the reason is not far to seek, for if it were ever admitted, then the whole structure of the relationship would be brought into question. This would create an intolerable situation. From the point of view of power, the stability of the order rests upon its total acceptance. To this end, the ancient role of the scapegoat is called into play. The mind of the South is temporarily incapable of dealing with dissatisfied and hostile restless Negroes. To admit this reality is to destroy the myth; to destroy the myth is to have all landmarks shift, making it impossible to hold one's course and keep one's bearings. Hence every effort has to be made to keep out the outsider and at the same time to open the way for the outsider to enter that he may be available to bear the brunt of the cause for unrest.

If the physical presence of the outsider is not available, then his influence may be blamed. Such influence flows into the common life because of the mobility of the segregated ones which may take them into other regions where the pattern is more fluid than in the South, or because of the enchantment with organizations that are based outside the region. It is not an accident that the attempt was made in Alabama, for instance, to declare an organization like the NAACP illegal in the state, or to label all the unrest and dissatisfaction as Communist inspired. It is this notion which, in part, accounts for the fact that again and again some white persons from other regions who settle in the South find themselves being more intensely anti-Negro than the native Southern white. If they are to share the common life, they must become a part of it so as not to seem to be outsiders and therefore a threat to the pattern. This is absolutely mandatory if one's livelihood is dependent upon harmonious relations with the people of the community. A way has to be found to blend with the landscape and become accepted if one is to survive.

Another device for dealing with the issue of unrest within the Negro community deep within the segregated pattern is to classify the white person as a "Nigger lover." In St. Augustine, Florida, during the turbulence of 1963, a newer phrase was used to apply to white persons who had rejected the pattern: "white Niggers." There the identification was complete and provision in the title made for the difference in skin coloring. The point here is that there is little ability to handle the fact that Negroes are rejecting the patterns upon which the social stability of the region rests. The rejection has to be rationalized so as to make the situation tolerable. Meanwhile, every measure must be taken to restore the orderly

10

way. The use of electric cattle prods, the turning of the full driving stream of water for fighting fires upon little children, defenseless girls, the dynamiting of a church resulting in the violent death of little children, the ambushing of men in cold blood, the brutalizing of vulnerable women in the stark desolation of jail cells—these are deeds of men with their backs against the wall; they are at *war*. And the stakes: the established pattern that is fading away. There is no preparation in mind or heart or culture for relating to Negroes outside of the segregated pattern.

Within this pattern, as has been suggested, it is possible for a white person to have some freedom of movement. He can make excursions beyond the barriers with real immunity. In my home town, white persons attended religious services in our church— but no Negro could attend services in a white church. One year I pumped the pipe organ for the organist to practice on at the Episcopal church. But on Sunday, at the service of worship, only a white boy could do this chore.

To be sure, when white persons attended our services, they were well-behaved, but they were present. I remember one Sunday some young people out on a lark came to our services. One of the fellows was not properly dressed. When the deacons tried to keep him from entering, he pushed his way into the service and we were all helpless to eject him because of the fear of reprisals. The following week he died suddenly from a heart attack and the word ran through the whole town that he was dead as an act of God.

Until very recently, then, the white person had certain large prerogatives which permitted him to disregard segregation or to honor it. More accurately, he was always under obligation to honor the pattern, but as a point of power privilege, he could disregard it on

11

occasion. That is the essential point to understand. In this matter he has enjoyed a unique privilege. He could move in and out of the Negro world without any major threat to the pattern.

●

The crisis set in motion by the Supreme Court Decision of 1954 introduced a radically new situation. To dishonor segregation has been pre-empted by Negroes as a right, not as a whim or a private prerogative. This decision, more than any other which the Court has rendered in the area of Civil Rights, created an entirely new issue for the South particularly. Why? Because it declared segregation itself to be unconstitutional. It made its declaration concerning the most critical seedbed for the perpetuation of the Southern pattern: the tax-supported public schools. It dealt with the fundamental responsibility of a society to educate the young, who in turn would become the responsible adults of the future. This is the taproot of the society and here it was declared that all children must be free to learn to live together with easy access to one another while the mind is developing and the heritage of the culture is being transmitted. The instinct to reject the decision sprang out of the profound awareness that it sounded the death gong for the pattern of segregation in all of its far-flung and complex dimensions.

The decision created a particularly traumatic experience for the man of good will in the white South. I mean the man who had a basic humanitarianism and who wanted the Negro to get the maximum fulfillment he could within the structure of the pattern. Such a person would be in favor of, and often would work for,

12

improvement of the schools, decent buildings, and adequate salaries for Negro teachers. He would give of his time and money in working to improve race relations. The period following hard upon the close of World War I marked the heyday of his activity. The work of the Southern Interracial Commission under the leadership of Dr. Will Alexander is a case in point. Here were men and women of definite good will and, for the period, of enlightened social concern. They took strong and often courageous positions against police brutality and the vastly inhuman treatment of helpless Negroes on the chain gangs in the South. Often in their private relations they associated with Negroes, not only because the experience was in itself satisfying but also because they were bearing witness to a real social concern. Included among these were certain groups within the churches of the South and particularly the Methodist Church, South, through its region-wide influential women's society.

But it must be kept in mind that all this activity took place within a framework which accepted and did not challenge the pattern. Even this behavior required a certain kind of courage which when looked at in the light of the present may not seem particularly significant. Always care was taken to get as much done as possible without challenging the pattern of segregation itself.

During the years when I was a teacher in Atlanta, I was invited to attend one of the meetings of the Interracial Commission. At the end of the morning session, I was beside myself with disgust. It seemed to me to be a waste of time and I could not accept the honesty and integrity of the Southern white people at the meeting. I was walking out of the door when one of the Negro college presidents stopped me to ask for my reaction. When I finished he said, "I understand how you feel, Thurman, but the thing that I keep saying to myself is that if we do not work with these people, there are no others in the South with whom we can work."

Later at one of the meetings I listened to one of the great liberal Southern Presbyterian preachers of Atlanta talk about the growth of the commission in its breadth of view. He told of the long and heated discussion concerning a question that had arisen when a world-famous Negro singer was coming to Atlanta for a concert in the city auditorium. Since the artist was Negro, it seemed too bad (and this was some growth) for the Negroes to be segregated in the customary balcony. The question was, "What shall we do with the Negroes if we permit them out of the balcony?" The predominant opinion was to have the Negroes sit in the very rear of the auditorium. The clergyman opposed that, and with tears running down his cheeks, he shared with the group a feeling of triumph when they divided the house perpendicularly rather than horizontally. Above all else the pattern must not be changed in any manner that is basic; it may be juggled, rearranged, but not changed.

But the fateful decision of the Court challenged the very foundations of the pattern. One of the inevitable heartbreaking effects is that the spirits and the souls of the children of the South are caught up in the struggle which really belongs to the adult world. Now for the first time in the South, white as well as Negro children are grappling with their environment as if they are adults. It is impossible even to imagine the kind of harvest that such a planting will bring forth. And yet the children left to themselves may not be so deeply scarred as one would think.

14

Betty Wisdom in her "Reflections on a Little Girl's Lunchbox" reveals some of the subtleties that are at work in the minds of teachers and students:

When the six-year-old girl first entered Frantz, one of the first two white grade schools in New Orleans to admit Negroes in 1960, nobody knew what to do with her. Nobody in the administration had laid down any rules of procedures for teachers and staff to follow. In the absence of direction from above, they did what was most natural for them: they established her in a classroom, insulated from the other children, with her own special teacher. When it came time for the other children to go downstairs to the cafeteria for lunch, she was kept entirely alone in her room to eat sandwiches she had brought from home. She only saw the other children when the school day was over, and then only from a distance. She didn't complain ever, and this state of things might have gone on indefinitely, if the children had not had a holiday on Thanksgiving.

During the holidays, the school staff always inspects the rooms and the children's lockers. When they came to her little locker, they found it full of sandwiches she was supposed to have been eating for lunch all those months. They saw then that the child was miserably unhappy and apprehensive, too apprehensive even to eat, but that to spare her mother the worry she would feel if she brought her lunch home uneaten, and to avoid the disapproval of the teachers if she threw her lunches away where they might be found, the little girl had hidden her daily sandwich in the only place that was all hers.

This thing, maybe a little thing, made the staff understand what a terrible burden they were imposing in isolating this child. They had, in fact, segregated her as though she were a carrier of disease.

From that time on, this little girl has been treated much like all

15

the other little girls in Frantz school. When school ended, the children presented a program, and she was naturally and unself-consciously a part of the program, and nobody thought twice about it.*

The Supreme Court decision did something else. The Southern white liberal could no longer work for improvement of conditions and relations between the two groups without taking a side either *for* the decision with its implications, or *against* the decision. He had to be on the side of the segregationists or the integrationists. He had no rallying point now for his good will. He was generally for the pattern of segregation, but he was no ardent segregationist. The growing edge of his social concern stopped short of doing away with segregation, but now he had no room in which to operate without casting his vote for the pattern, absolutely. There was no dependable voice in the region that had sufficient moral power to speak as one aware *of* the pattern but not affected *by* the pattern. And there was no one outside the region who had the right to speak and not be regarded as an outsider with all that the term connoted in the contemporary psychology. Someone must be found who could speak the clear word on behalf of the nation as a whole and who would make the claim effectively that the South was a part of the United States and make the claim stick. The figure would have to be one who had the political right into which a moral content could be placed.

The obvious person would be the President of the United States who by our system, once he is elected, becomes the President of all the people and who in matters affecting the common welfare is beyond party affiliations, even those of the party whose standard-bearer he was in the popular election. At first it seemed to be a

* From *The New South*, November 1961, p. 14. Used by permission.

fortunate moment for the country because the man who was President had a national image unique in our history—an image which placed him above the tensions and struggles of party politics. Such a President, if he spoke out on the side of the decision, would provide a rallying point, particularly for the white liberals of the South. But there was, in essence, a profound and abiding silence! In the *New York Times Magazine* of August 30, 1964, there is a letter written by an ex-Southerner and a Caucasian who makes essentially the same case:

In a free society no law can long endure unless it is accepted in the hearts of men. But the hearts of men can be more receptive to laws about which they have doubts if those in positions of authority will exert the moral leadership which their office provides.

To offer an embarrassing example, even convinced segregationists were ready to follow the Supreme Court decisions of 1954, had President Eisenhower, then at the zenith of his prestige, seen fit to exert the moral authority of his office. Only the Presidency could have acted to assure swift and cheerful compliance, for (as events have subsequently proved) convinced Southern liberals were relatively few and disorganized and the moderates, as usual, would tend to be swayed by the most eloquent spokesmen.

It was hoped and expected that the President would call a conference of Southern Governors and urge them to work out peaceful procedures by which the decisions could be put into effect, smoothly and consistently and without tension. But no conference was called, and no Presidential action was taken until the Little Rock crisis. By that time the hard-core segregationists had had a chance to perfect their organization and intimidate the believers in obedience to law.

Thus the liberals in the South, for the most part, had to run to cover, leaving the field wide open for the doctrinaire segregationists. For a while they carried the day, and even as these words are written, they are holding the line in important ways even though at many levels there is the crumbling of resistance.

●

We come back now to a discussion of the new element in the attack on the pattern of segregation, the pre-empting of the *right* to dishonor and disregard segregation. In the past, certain members of white society could and often did ignore segregation. They could break its rules as a point of personal privilege as white persons. Whenever that happened, it was scarcely construed as a basic attack on the pattern, but rather as an idiosyncrasy or, at best, as an individual protest. Such persons were not responding to the appeal of a higher law, were not being obedient to the demands of a religious conviction or a spiritual commitment, but for reasons sometimes personal, sometimes obscure, they were taking full advantage of their position as white persons. There was a short period in the South when a small group *defied* the pattern allegedly because of revolutionary political convictions.

At the present time, when white persons are ignoring the pattern of segregation and participating in the struggle against it on so many levels because of moral convictions or in response to religious commitment, it is not easy for the behavior to be taken at face value by Negroes. The longer the white persons persist, involving themselves in all the attendant risks, the more credible their position becomes, and the more they are trusted. It is a cruel burden that none can share. What a difference there would have been in the long night deep in the pit made secure by segregation had increasing

18

numbers of white persons disregarded segregation continuously in the name of democracy, morality, Jesus Christ or the prophets of Israel, or some other profound spiritual imperative! Instead what we have seen historically is the general pattern in which to disregard segregation has been a "privilege" of the white man in a society which he dominated. Otherwise, for the most part in the present crisis he would have a voice clear and strong rather than what often seems the agonizing cry of guilt and ruptured conscience. In one of Petrarch's Letters of Old Age appear these words:

When a word must be spoken to further a good cause, and those whom it behooves to speak remain silent, anybody ought to raise his voice, and break a silence which may be fraught with evil. . . . Many a time a few simple words have helped further the welfare of the nation, no matter who uttered them; the voice itself displaying its latent powers, sufficed to move the hearts of men.

The ancient "right" of persons in the white society to honor or to dishonor segregation as it fits their needs or whims is being challenged by Negro persons and by some white persons. The white persons who act now are doing so deliberately. The casual violation of the pattern has disappeared. This fact is worthy of compelling emphasis. Let us assess precisely what is happening. Until very recently and in connection with the creative surge on behalf of civil rights, any infringement on the pattern of segregation was an indulgence of the prerogative of power. Very rarely indeed did the Negro figure in this because he was completely exposed to attack from all sides. It is true that over the years there were isolated instances of Negroes defying or ignoring the pattern. The exceptions merely dramatized the awful consistency of the pattern itself.

The phenomenon of groups and individual Negroes deliberately

19

choosing to disregard segregation even in the most reactionary sections of the South is a new experience for them and for the country as a whole. The civil rights movement precipitated an opening which made it possible for Negroes to participate in it and thereby recapture and/or establish initiative over their own lives. At last any one of them could do something on behalf not only of the rest of them but of the larger society. One is reminded of the words from the Sermon on the Mount: "If a man slaps you on one cheek, turn the other cheek." That is to say, if this happens to you, don't take it, but do something. Turn the other cheek.

In addition the choice of disregarding segregation is an exercise of an inherent right as American citizens. It is important that they are not doing this merely as Negroes on their own behalf, but as American citizens on behalf of all citizens. Thereby do they point up that segregation is a violation of the human spirit and contrary to the integrity of the Constitution which broods over the total life of the country as the spirit of the hive broods over the apiary. The position must be seen in its clarity. All the various contemporary pressures against the "walls that divide" that have arisen within the Negro community are in fact individual and collective efforts to render null and void the very structure of the pattern of segregation. These efforts are an expression of social and moral responsibility for the total society, and not an exercise of the authority or whim of status and privilege. Now it is possible for a white person who chooses to ignore the pattern to become involved profoundly in a movement to redeem his society. He is not acting primarily as a Christian or a Jew, as a white person, as a Republican or a Democrat, but as a citizen who is asserting his sense of responsibility for the total life of the society. The right to act as a result of religious conviction is a right that has been forfeited and has to be reclaimed. Whether this can be done, no one can say.

To exercise a civic right is a live option and provides the broadest possible basis for operation. I do not wish to suggest that there are not many who are participating in the social struggle inspired to do so by deep religious convictions. But my insistence is that the church has lost the initiative to inspire such behavior in our society. The image of the church is so damaged that at the moment it does not provide an effective rallying point.

●

It is a great irony that the Negro church has figured so largely as a rallying center for the civil rights movement in the South primarily because of its strategic position as an institution in Negro life; it has not become a civil rights rallying center because of its religious ethical teaching as such. But the logic of the impact of the religious experience in the Negro church made it inevitable that it would become such a center. For a long time the Negro church was the one place in the life of the people which was comparatively free from interference by the white community. A man may be buffeted about by his environment, or may be regarded as a nobody in the general community; a woman may be a nurse in a white family in which the three-year-old child in her care calls her by her first name, thus showing quite unconsciously the contempt in which she is held by his parents. When this Negro man and this Negro woman come to their church, however, for one terribly fulfilling moment they are somebody.

Perhaps this immunity from interference and violence which the

Negro church enjoyed until recent times was owing not to reverence or respect for the religious institution as such but perhaps to superstition. One day a friend of mine, who was a clergyman, and I were driving in the downtown section of a Southern city. We were so engrossed in conversation that my friend, who was driving the car, drove through a red light without seeing it. The white policeman on the corner blew his whistle and ran up behind us, ordering my friend to pull over. He came around to the driver's seat, swearing violently, pulled out his billy and reached into the open window of the car to grab my friend by the neck to make his head available for cracking. My friend looked him in the eye and said very quietly, "You would not hit a man of God, would you, officer?" The policeman froze, muttered something, and ended up telling him to drive on. It may be that here was at work an ancient taboo which gave to the religious immunity from interference so as not to offend the gods.

When I was a student in Atlanta, a blind Negro was killed by a policeman. Feeling ran high all through the Negro community. When his funeral was held, officers of the law, fearing that it would be an occasion for some kind of uprising, came to the service but remained outside the church. In his sermon, the minister had only words of consolation to give to the family. In his prayer to God, he expressed his anger and hostility toward the white community. He could do this in a prayer without exposing the Negro community to retaliation.

This whole picture has changed almost overnight since the Negro church became the overt center for rallying the spirit of Negroes. Thus churches are bombed, burned, and generally are under constant attack and pressure.

It is a curious phenomenon that the personality who has played a major part in the inspiration for nonviolent action is not Thoreau, or Whittier, or even Tolstoi, but a man from an entirely different culture and an entirely different faith: Mahatma Gandhi. One wonders deeply about the meaning of this fact. However, the image of the citizen who is acting as one who maintains in himself a sense of responsibility for the fate of his country is a compelling one and one capable of making the large and imperative demand. Men have always been able to rally when the very life of the nation is at stake. It can be argued that the enthusiasm engendered, the call to sacrifice, the sense of participation in a collective destiny that involves the total nation—all these have a religious dimension, but it is outside of the religious institution. And that is my point.

The thing that made the deepest impression on me at the ceremonies at the base of the Lincoln Monument on the day of the March on Washington in 1963, was not the vast throng, as thrilling as it was to be a part of such a tremendous movement of peoples on the march; it was not the inspired oratory of all the participating speakers, including the dazzling magic of the music and utter vitality springing from the throat of Martin Luther King; it was not the repeated refrain of Eugene Blake, saying on behalf of the church, we are late but we are here—no, it was none of these things. What impressed me most was a small group of young people representing student nonviolent groups, fresh from the jails and violences of the South, who time and time again caught the spiritual overtones of the speakers and led the critical applause which moved like a tidal wave over the vast audience. I do not know but this observation may be an embarrassment to them, but this is how it seemed to

23

me. These young people were tuned to the spiritual dimension of what they were about even as what they were about was the exercising of their civic rights inherent in their citizenship.

The real evil of segregation is the imposition of self-rejection! It settles upon the individual a status which announces to all and sundry that he is of limited worth as a human being. It rings him round with a circle of shame and humiliation. It binds his children with a climate of no-accountness as a part of their earliest experience of the self. Thus it renders them cripples, often for the length and breadth of their days. And for this there is no forgiveness, only atonement. And only God can judge of what that atonement consists. What does it mean to grow up with a cheap self-estimate? There is a sentence I copied many years ago, the source of which I have forgotten: "We were despised so long at last we despised ourselves."

I think this is the root of what seems to be the careless regard that Negroes sometimes have for their own lives and the lives of their fellows. It is extraordinarily difficult to see day after day your life and the life of your fellows cheaply held, to be born and to live in the midst of a climate of violence without being deeply affected by it. Added to this is the fact that little note is made of the taking of a Negro's life at the hands of a Negro, which says that the law itself does not view the taking of the life of one's fellows as particularly worthy of punishment. When the whole world in which one lives is stripped of respect for persons, the mind, the thoughts, and the spirit are poisoned.

Irreverence for persons has to be separated in one's thinking from the old fear of violence, which fear has been the weapon in the hands of the so-called masters of the environment. It may be that we are in the throes of a vast paradox. Life cheaply considered in the environment tends to cause those whose lives are so regarded to deal with their fellows in ways that reflect the same attitudes. And yet beyond this there is the fear of mindless and nonprovocative violence. It would seem that the threat of violence can create fear that paralyzes and freezes. Thus there has to be in the ground of one's thinking the subtle but pervasive distinction between the fact of violence and the threat of violence. The threat of violence opens up the Pandora's box of the imagination and may be far more deleterious than violence itself. Even the promise of violence postponed is apt to be more unmanageable than violence itself. It was harder for me to manage the promise of a whipping by my mother than the whipping itself when it came along.

●

As long as Negroes functioned within the pattern, the fear of reprisal and punitive measures was a very effective deterrent. The fear was always current and always active. It could be implemented quickly anywhere by any white man. To use violence as a deterrent against the violation of the pattern had a general sanction in the white community. And the surest protection against its use was not one's guilt or innocence but rather one's cunning or the protection of some white man who stood in the gate on your behalf. The stability of the pattern rested uneasily on the active fear of the Negro. The fear, in turn, was based on the threat and the fact of violence and the inactive fear of the white man, which sprang from his deep unconscious guilt because of his treatment of the Negro and his genuine anxiety about the security of his own position and

25

status. The active fear of the Negro and the inactive fear of the white man provided a condition of tension that stabilized the pattern of segregation. The behavior pattern involved made it possible for each to function automatically within the "zones of agreement."

Now a strange thing is happening, particularly in the South. The active fear in the Negro, one of the foundation stones providing uneasy stability for segregation, is rapidly disappearing. It is difficult to assess this phenomenon with accuracy. It seems to me that the fear of the threat of violence as a deterrent is rapidly being replaced by an increasing sense of personal and inner freedom. The more Negroes lose their fear, the more white people increase their fear. Thus a person can act within the tight insistence of his sense of personal civic responsibility. In other words, he is released to be himself as a citizen. His increasing loss of his fear activates the latent fear of white persons in the region. When both are free of the fear, then a new way of life opens for all—but I must not run ahead of my argument. May it be remembered that the cost to the perpetrator of segregation is a corrosion of the spirit and the slow deadly corruption of the soul. It is to be overcome by evil.

The son of a prominent Southern white businessman, while studying abroad in the twenties, met a Negro who was president of a college in his home town. The student wrote letters to his father about his new and wonderful friend—an educated refined Negro gentleman who reminded him very much of his father. After much correspondence and what else must be left to the imagination, the son succeeded in getting his father to agree to invite the Negro college president to his home for dinner. Elaborate protections were provided: the dinner was scheduled for nine o'clock in the evening; the Negro servants were given the

26

night off so that they would not know what was going on. What must have been the agony of conflict in the bosom of that father who wanted to be true to the image which his son had of him, to be true to his own sense of integrity in encounter with a man of equal stature, and at the same time to do nothing that would disturb the pattern of segregation which was a part of his very peace of mind! The cost was the corrosion of the spirit, which is slow and imperceptible—but its effect is sure and relentless.

When I was an undergraduate in Atlanta, I worked as a messenger for the dean's office. My position was in a chair in the outer office. One day a local salesman came in to see the dean. While he was waiting, we talked. At length the question of race came up. The salesman explained to me why he was not rearing his children to hate Negroes. "Don't misunderstand me, boy," he said, "I don't 'love' Negroes and certainly don't want my children to love them. But that is not the same as hating them. Hate is a funny thing. It does not have a mind. All hate knows to do is to hate. If I teach my children to hate Negroes, they may end up hating white people too—and I can't run the risk of ruining their lives in that way."

In order to overcome the ravages of segregation, the overt sufferers must carry on an energy-consuming inner struggle which undermines their effectiveness in practically every aspect of their lives. Such persons tend to be emotionally exhausted as a chronic state of being. There is the barest margin for creativity and growth. It is impossible even to hazard the loss to American life that has resulted from the waste in energy and creativity in the desperate necessity to find a way to survive against such overwhelming odds. I speak here primarily of mental and emotional energy.

One of my friends, who is a sociologist, was to attend a meeting

27

of the Southern Sociological Association in a downtown hotel. He was scheduled to read a paper at the opening session at nine-thirty. When he arrived, finally, at the meeting place, he sat for a few minutes to rest and gather himself. Presently he was joined by a white sociologist who said to my friend, "The day hasn't started and you look bushed already." The reply was, "By the time I arrived up here on this floor for the meeting, I had gone through enough emotional waste with doormen, bellboys, elevator operators and passengers to render a normal man a nervous wreck, and in five minutes I must read a paper to a group of men who have no understanding of what it cost me to get here to read the paper."

Of course, it must never be forgotten that again and again one's physical life is at stake as well. This was brought home to me very graphically one day when I was a visitor on a Negro college campus in Texas. It was a church-related college. During that particular year there had been a large number of suicides among American college students. At a discussion group led by a white representative of the board of the church operating the school, he asked the students to account for the fact that Negro students were not a part of this "movement to suicide." After much talk, pro and con, one student offered the comment, "Negro students must spend so much energy in keeping white people from killing them that they do not have much left with which to take their own lives." There was general laughter to cover the sense of embarrassment and nakedness which such an exposure revealed.

●

How does the human spirit accommodate itself to desolation? How has this been achieved within Negro life through all the weary years of segregation and its devastating implications? There is a kind of immunity that comes from putting all white persons in a separate category and functioning within the boundaries of Negro life as if they did not exist. This is to accept segregation. An aspect of this has been referred to in the early part of this essay. The spirit does with the literal fact of the existence of white persons what the body does with an infection. A thick wall is built around the infected area in an attempt to prevent the spread of the infection into the rest of the system to poison and destroy it. The body functions with health so long as there is no breach in the wall. The basis of all the movements of separation within the group, the effort to maintain as nearly as possible a completely bi-racial society, to be two parallel lines that may meet only in infinity—all such notions are rooted in the necessity for finding and achieving immunity from the perilous involvement with white persons.

When I was dean of Rankin Chapel at Howard University, one of our visiting Negro clergymen preached a sermon, using as his text, "If thou be a great people, then get thee up to the wood country, and cut down for thyself there in the land of the Perizzites and of the giants, if mount Ephraim be too narrow for thee" (Josh. 17:15).* The ideal situation which he presented to the students was one in which all authority and power would be within the group itself. After all these years, I can still hear him say, "I want Negro policemen, I want Negro jails, if I am to be hanged, I want a Negro gallows. . . ." This is a form of charisma that always has a certain appeal to those who suffer from consensus of rejection which segregation symbolizes. The fact that such separatism is not a practical procedure, that it cuts one off from the

* The paraphrase quoted by the minister was, "If the borders of Ephraim be too narrow for thee, go ye out into the wilderness and hew down a place for yourself."

basic right to be a part of the common life, that it is falling away from the sense of participation in a collective destiny—all these are often forgotten.

Within Negro life there are important monuments to the position. Negro business enterprises, Negro churches, etc., are all rooted in this kind of response to social necessity. It provides for a sense of belonging to and of counting in that tends to counterbalance segregation. The social significance is to provide compensation for being forced to live behind walls. It establishes identity and confers persona upon individuals. It makes for the feeling of being "at home." But most important, it exploits whatever there is of an ethnic idiom. And this is good, very good. Such grounding of personal dignity gives to individuals a sense of center which in turn serves as a foil for the threatening impact of the hostility and indifference of the larger community. With this kind of inner reinforcement, it is possible for the ego structure to withstand the shattering impact of the wider rejection.

At the close of a lecture before the Nigerian Press Club in Ibadan, I was asked by one of the members, "What is your personal reaction to the separatist movement in your country which is in fact the acceptance of segregation?" I said, "There is a recognition that given segregation, a way developed by which use could be made of it to keep alive the dignity of people who were so treated. But there is a real danger inherent in accepting segregation: it could very easily cause people to feel that they are *aliens* in their own country. Once an American feels that America is not his homeland, he has given up his right to claim the fruits of citizenship. This right must be maintained at all costs because if it is lost within the spirits of Negroes, then the door to citizenship closes within his

30

own heart. It would mean that the external denial of citizenship as expressed in segregation becomes internalized and all is lost."

In 1927 I was en route to Houston from the east coast. It was necessary for me to change trains at one-thirty in the morning at a junction point in Texas. I was the only person getting off. As I walked toward the Jim Crow station, out of nowhere a Negro man appeared by my side, walking in step. He asked me if I were changing trains or getting off there. Before I could answer him he said, "I have been meeting all the trains during the night to let any colored people who may be coming here or laying over know that the whole town is in an uproar. Late this afternoon a sheriff was killed and it is dangerous for any Negro to be seen on the streets after dark. If you take my advice, you will go and sit in the waiting room in full view with your suitcase by you so that if any white men come through here they will know that you are a stranger waiting for the next train. If you ask the ticket agent a question and he acts as if he didn't hear you, don't ask him a second time. You might get in trouble."

At length I grew tired of waiting in the stuffy station and decided to sit in the open door on the steps with the light from the room falling straight across me, and with my suitcase in front of me. After some minutes I became aware of the presence of another person. Then I heard a voice say, "Now about the Democratic primary, the time is going to come when that 'Nigra' dentist who is taking the case to the Supreme Court might win and if he wins it means breaking the back of the Democratic primary in the State of Texas because the 'Nigra' will have the vote. I think this would be a terrible thing because it is all that decent people like me [he himself had the general appearance of a tramp] can do to

31

keep the white riff-riff from using the vote to upset everything. If you add the 'Nigra' vote to that, they will drive the rest of us into the Gulf of Mexico.

"But you know what I would do if I was a 'Nigra' [by this time he was standing almost in front of me]? Every time the white people had their primary, I would set up 'Nigra' voting places in every church, every lodge, every restaurant, poolroom, and barbershop. I would print the same kind of ballot that the white people are using. I would see to it that every one of my people voted on the same candidates. When the voting was over, the ballots would be counted and burned up and you know why I would do this— so that all the 'Nigras' would get the habit of voting. If they did this, as soon as the Supreme Court opened the door, they would be ready to step right in, but if they are not ready to step in, by the time they get ready, we would have found another way to close the door."

●

One of the other dangers of the acceptance of segregation is difficult to verbalize. It is to have a feeling that the withdrawal of segregation is a privilege which the white community may confer upon Negroes and of which they must prove themselves worthy. It is extremely hard to resist such a mood. Actually, segregation inspires, aids, and abets it. It has not been uncommon to have some Negroes say, as they are observing a lack of decorum or good behavior on the part of their fellows, "Sometimes, I don't blame white people for segregating Negroes." This attitude is an invidious and deadly one, for it assumes that the presumptive

32

right of white people who are in a position of power to segregate and thereby exercise control over Negro life is an inherent right. Thus the burden rests always on the shoulders of the Negro to prove himself worthy "to integrate." He is in the psychologically defensive position of acknowledging "squatter's rights" as rights "in fee simple." In other words, the Negro must prove that he is as good as a white man and is therefore entitled to all the rights, privileges, and perquisites vouchsafed to the white man in the society in which he has the power of veto and certification. Such an attitude can develop without one's realizing it until some moment of dramatic awareness manifests it.

This position is further aided by many well-meaning white persons. Not long ago on the train, a man sitting across from me in the diner said, "Now that the Civil Rights Bill has passed, I hope you people will prove worthy of the privileges granted." He was quite unprepared for my reaction. I had to explain to him what his attitude implied about the meaning of the rights. He equated rights under the social contract as expressed in law, in so far as they were enjoyed by Negroes, with privileged rights conferred by the white community and for which Negroes must be both worthy and grateful.

No wonder the notion is abroad that the price that must be paid for release from the prison of segregation is the surrender of everything that has been meaningful and significant in Negro life under the pattern of segregation. What one has discerned to be indigenous and of timeless value during the long period of enforced separation must be denied in the new order of relatedness. There is something utterly false about this. It is a denial of the integrity and the experience of life.

Negro students in the South during the second and third decades of this century met annually in YM and YWCA conferences at King's Mountain, North Carolina. It was there that the religious leadership was funded and out of that place a long procession of men and women moved onto the scene of American life inspired and dedicated both to the cause of religion and to a socially healthy society. Many attempts were made to bring together the white conference, which met at Blue Ridge, and the King's Mountain conference, resulting in one united intergroup conference. All through the years of negotiation and experimentation with fraternal delegates, the common assumption was that the Negro conference would, in the very nature of the case, give up the things that had made King's Mountain so influential in the lives of students of those generations. Without question the first thing to give up was the meeting place itself. The fact that the multiplication of meaningful experiences at a single spot through the years would have to be assessed and taken into account was not given any consideration. To be sure, Blue Ridge had superior appointments and facilities; it had the prestige of being a white conference ground. White students would not give up their meeting place made sacred and hallowed by the vision beatific. No. They were only asked to make room for the Negroes. That was for them a great deal.

The simple observation I am making is that that specific situation merely reflected the general assumption that the Negro must be worthy and therefore must win the right to become a normal part of American society. Such a presupposition is essentially false and is a distortion of the concept of citizenship.

There are varying versions of a story going the rounds to illustrate the basic idea. Here is the story: A Negro went into an

34

"integrated" restaurant to get a meal. The waitress brought him the menu. After he had read it carefully, he looked up at her to say,

"Do you have any collard greens?"

"No sir."

"Do you have any pigs' feet or pigs' tails?"

"No sir."

"Do you have any mustard greens and corn bread?"

"No sir."

"Well," he said, "you folks aren't ready for integration."

When the New York World's Fair opened and there was the threat of a "stall-in" in the arterial highways leading to the Fair, there was general alarm and consternation. Such activity from civil rights workers would be irresponsible and could not and should not be condoned. But when such behavior was held as proof that Negroes did not deserve civil rights, that it would create an unyielding mood, causing white persons to withdraw their willingness to grant civil rights to Negroes, the whole civil rights issue was thrown out of focus.

Civil rights are not a gift bestowed upon "good" Negroes, upon well-behaved Negroes, upon Negroes who have been accepted by white persons as worthy recipients of civil rights. No! They are essential rights which are the common heritage of all citizens. It is only an incident of the historic moment that places within the sanction of a dominant majority in the country the power to exercise veto or certification in the granting of rights. This privilege of power is deeply embedded in the consciousness of the American people. It has been the key to the relationship between the races for generations and it is difficult to be uprooted. For the Negro, it tends to make him seem to himself to be a beggar seeking a grace from white society. For white society or white persons, it makes them seem to themselves to be the sole judge of who should and who should not be granted the rights and the responsibilities of citizenship.

The immigrant who comes to this country seeking a new home soon realizes the psychology of this attitude. The sooner he accepts the dominant mood, the sooner will he be accepted, not as a foreigner but as a white American. And this is the point. The more insecure he feels himself to be as a newcomer, the more quickly does he fit into the general attitudes of the white community toward Negroes. That he may have been the victim of racial, religious, or political persecution in his homeland does not matter. The general tendency is for him to make his place in the new world secure by ingratiating himself to the white community as a *white* man in good standing.

Some years ago when I devoted a part of a summer serving as one of the lecturers in a series of international institutes conducted by the Quakers, I had a chance to observe the anatomy of the process by which a newcomer to the country seeks to make his place secure with the white community. At a lecture given by such a person—in this case the man happened to be a German— at a small Midwestern college, he told the following story: The upstairs maid in a certain home answered the telephone: "Yes— yes—it certainly is," and hung up. Whereupon she said to the lady of the house, "Some lady on the phone wanted to know if this was the residence of Mrs. Smith. When I said 'yes' then she wanted to know if Mrs. Smith was at home and I said, 'yes.' Then she made a funny remark, 'It's a long distance from New York,' and I answered 'it certainly is' and hung up."

36

The lecturer was quite a prestigious person to the Midwesterners attending the institute. For the most part they were teachers and community leaders who were concerned about broadening their understanding of Europe and European life. The guest lecturer was quite a hero among them and in their attitude he was lionized.

When we moved on to Portland, Oregon, there was a chill in the atmosphere regarding the propriety of having a German lecturer. One of the daily papers had carried an editorial that was not particularly friendly to the presence of the lecturer. When he gave his first lecture, at the appropriate place in his discussion he told the same story with this difference. Instead of saying "yes" he said "yes ma'am." Instead of saying "it certainly is" he said, "it shure is," imitating as carefully as he could a Negro dialect.

But when we moved on to northern California, to Oakland, the atmosphere was definitely hostile toward him. In fact, the executives of the institute had been visited by a protest group. Even the radio broadcast that the lecturer was scheduled to give had to be canceled. He became the outsider trying to get in. What had been acceptance became rejection. And what did he do? I was curious so I attended his lecture, hearing it now for the third time. At the appropiate place in his discussion he told the same story but with this drastic difference—the maid was identified as a *Negro* maid.

It was clear that as the lecturer became increasingly threatened in his position of acceptance as a white man, he sought to reassure the white persons of his "all rightness" by implying "we are all the same; I am a white person like you and to prove it, my attitude toward Negroes is the same as yours." To this day, I am not sure that he was aware of what he was doing!

37

The acceptance of the fact and the status of segregation has the ramifications outlined above and many more. It is sufficient to summarize the section by saying that such acceptance is to be regarded as being, and/or to regard one's self as being, a nonmember of society. It is to resign one's sense of membership in the society. It is to yield to a gross evil.

●

Or the human spirit may deal with the fact and the status of segregation by active and positive resentment. Ultimately, such resentment often becomes a substantial residue in the spirit. The most accurate designation of such a residue is hate. There is something cold and deliberate and passionless about hate of this kind. It is what is left when the active ferment of resentment and bitterness has been exhausted.

In a book which I wrote in 1946 under the title of *Jesus and the Disinherited*, there appeared an analysis of hate which I shall use now as the basis of my discussion. The setting for hate often begins in situations where there are contacts without fellowship. That is, contacts that are devoid of the simple overtones of warmth, fellow-feeling, and genuineness. There is some region in every man that listens for the sound of the genuine in other men. But where there is contact that is stripped of fellow-feeling, the sound cannot come through and the will to listen for it is not manifest. What happens behind the walls of segregation when the reaction to segregation is positive resentment and bitterness? I am not unmindful that there can be and often is an abundance of sentimentality masquerading under the cloak of fellowship. I am

38

remembering also that all through the years there have been isolated experiences of genuine fellowship. Even in the South the walls of segregation were sometimes transcended and a person behind the walls listened for and heard the sound of the genuine in the person on the other side. But this is rare.

It is not too difficult to have fellowship on your own terms if you are in a position of power and to repudiate it if your terms are rejected. In the South, as long as the Negro is called John or Mary and seems to accept the profoundly humiliating position of an inferior status, fellowship within the zones of agreement is possible. It has not been uncommon for great personal sacrifices to be made for Negroes and all the weight of personal position and power put at their disposal. But always this has been done within the zones of agreement established and assured by the mutual horizon of the pattern. It is precisely because of this false basis of fellowship so often occurring that in the section of the country where there is the greatest contact between the races, there is apt to be the least real fellowship and the first step along the terrible road of bitterness and hate is assured. One of the common elements present in town after town since the deeply unsettled conditions emerged in the South is the complete breakdown of communication between the Negro and the white community. Communication is possible only where the agendas are the same. When the status is mutually accepted, this makes for a common agenda upon which communication takes place. When this is no longer true, the agendas become different and communication breaks down.

Contacts without fellowship tend to express themselves in unsympathetic understanding. To be sure, there is understanding of a certain kind, but it is without the healing and reinforcement of

39

personality. The energy and spirit of the persons involved are not available to each other. It is like the experience of going to a man's office to be interviewed for a job. In that stripping moment before being seated, when the full gaze of the other person is focused upon you, suddenly you wonder if your tie is crooked, or if one of the buttons on your shirt is missing, but you dare not look to find out. In such a penetrating, incisive, cold understanding there is no cushion to absorb limitations or to provide extenuating circumstances for protection.

When a man says, "I understand," he may mean something kind, warm, and gracious. But there is an understanding that is cold, hard, minute, and devastating. It is the kind of understanding that one gives to the enemy, or that is derived from an accurate knowledge of another's power to injure. There is the understanding of another's weakness, which may be used as a weapon of defense or offense. Often when the Southern white person says, "I understand the Negro," what he really means is that he has a knowledge of the Negro within the limitations and boundaries which the white man has established. The kind of Negro he understands has little existence in reality except as an image in his own mind.

Unsympathetic understanding is very easily activated into ill will. It may be quite an unconscious step or movement of the spirit. It may be a general or pervasive mood which influences the character of casual encounters or it may inform, quite intentionally, the pointed, face-to-face encounter. It breeds suspicion and inspires many little acts of no-faith. It creates an all-encompassing climate. This unsympathetic understanding may make the Negro say, "No white man can be trusted," or it may make the white person say, "All Negroes are liars and thieves." It makes the areas of contact

40

become a no man's land where men move around as shadows in a world of shadows.

Hate is the residue when the ferment is through churning and only an irreducible constituent remains. To make my idea very clear, suppose you were one of five children in a family and it happened again and again that if there was just enough for four children in a given circumstance, you were the child who had to do without. If there was money for four pairs of shoes and five pairs were needed, it was you who did without shoes. If there were five pieces of cake on the plate, four healthy slices and one small piece, you were given the small slice. At first when this happened you were scarcely aware of it because you thought each of your brothers and sisters would have his turn for the short end of the stick; but this did not ever seem to be the case. You complained quietly to the brother who was closest to you in understanding, and he thought you were being oversensitive or actually disloyal to your mother and father for harboring such thoughts. In a moment of indignation or outrage you spoke to your father about it. You were amazed that he seemed completely incapable of understanding your attitude and chastised you because you were not grateful for your place in the family. You decided not to mention the matter again, but now you kept on watching and checking. The unfairness continued.

At night, when the lights were out and you were safely tucked away in bed, you would reach down into the quiet places of your little heart and lift out your bundles of resentments and bitternesses growing out of the family situation. These you fingered tenderly in the darkness. One by one you held them until you could feel the inner quality of their hurt. In the darkness you muttered to

41

yourself, "They can keep me from talking about it to them, but they can't keep me from resenting it. I despise them for what they are doing to me. No one can prevent me there." Bitterness and resentment slowly distill into hate.

As long as the emotion is active, there is deep inner agitation, conflict, and turmoil. The feeling tone is acute and dynamic. Things are movable and the behavior is mobile. There is always the chance that something positive and creative may result in a kind of truce of reconciliation. Something may get through that may be healing and redemptive.

The real danger to the health of the personality comes when all stirrings and ferment cease. One day, as I was returning to college, I stopped to warm myself by a fire at the bottom of the hill called Beaver's Slide. A group of Negro men were warming themselves and discussing some recent situation in which they were involved. At length one young man picked up his ukelele and began strumming an accompaniment to a blues, the refrain of which was "Been down so long, down don' worry me." He had landed on the other side of ferment and active hostility. In one sense he was beyond the strength to care. It is this quality that is present when hostility, resentment, and bitterness are drained away and only hate, devoid of all elements of positive caring, is left. There is something that is utterly desolate about this. A pathological detachment becomes possible and the individual seems to have no feeling capability as far as the object and the cause of his hostility are concerned.

Two incidents come to mind separated from each other by a quarter of a century. One involved how the residue may be transmitted to children in a most terrifying manner. I was seated in a Jim Crow car at a railway station in Texas. Two Negro girls, about

42

fourteen or fifteen years old, sat directly behind me. One of them looked out of the window and said, "Look at those kids." She referred to two little white girls who were skating down the highway toward the train. "Wouldn't it be funny if they fell and spattered their brains all over the pavement!" I looked back at them. Through what torture chambers had they come—torture chambers that had so attacked the grounds of humaneness in them —that there was nothing capable of calling forth any appreciation or understanding of white persons! There was something that made me shiver.

The other took place at a meeting of a Negro civic organization in the Deep South. When I entered the meeting and took my seat in the back of the church, I recognized that the man who was addressing the group was a minister. He was reporting to the group an experience he had that afternoon when he was visiting one of his parishioners in the local hospital. He said that while he was in the Negro ward, a white patient was rolled into the ward because he had an illness that temporarily had defied accurate diagnosis. Since the doctors could not determine whether or not his illness was contagious, they did not want to take any chance that his illness might be spread to the other white patients. Until that could be determined, he was placed in the Negro ward, just in case.

A low moan went up from various parts of the auditorium. Then very dramatically a man arose and apologetically asked if he could make a statement that might be helpful. Permission was granted. This is the story that he told.

"One day my friend John was walking down the street near the Loop in Chicago. He had four quarters in his pocket, the sum total of all the money he had. He saw a white man seated on the curb, begging from the passersby. The man was a pitiful object—both legs were cut off near his waist. He had no arms and one eye was opaque with blindness. When John saw the man, he emptied his pockets of the four quarters and gave them all to the beggar. The beggar said, 'God bless you,' whereupon John said, 'Mister, that is all the money I have. If I had any more I would certainly give it to you.'

" 'Thank you. Thank you very much. But I am puzzled that you are willing to give me *all* the money you have. Why?'

"It was then that John said to him, 'You are the first white man I have ever seen that is cut up the way a white man deserves to be cut up that the least I can do to show my thanks is to give you my last dollar.' "

There was laughter in the group but it was laughter in a house of the dead.

There is a dynamic quality in the residue which points up the paradox of hate. Hatred may become a foundation upon which the personality stands in an effort to establish a dreadful emotional security. It is possible for a personal significance to emerge on the other side of hate that becomes a form of self-validation. As such it is so intensely personal and private that it becomes a fortress for the ego structure. For a limited and on occasion extended time interval the individual seems to be impregnable. When this happens the very hatred itself becomes an internal rallying center for the personality. The energy generated may be regarded as the strength of a kind of neurosis. Surplus energy is created and placed at the disposal of the individual's needs and ends. The whole

44

personality seems to be alerted. All kinds of supports for implementing one's affirmed or confirmed position are seized upon. A strange new cunning possesses the mind, and every opportunity for taking advantage, for defeating, for striking out against the enemy is revealed in clear perspective. An amazing quality of endurance emerges. It must never be forgotten that hate has an endurance capability in what it may inspire the human spirit to suffer and to sustain.

Nevertheless the essential evil of hate manifests itself in two deadly ways. Despite the fact that there is a hard core of ego refuge or foundation, ultimately and perhaps sooner, hate withers the spirit in a terrible isolation. It provides a bitter fruit upon which to feed and slowly it poisons the whole being. In my boyhood there was a common belief that during the month of August when the rattlesnake is changing his skin, he is apt to poison himself. The way we put it, the coach whip (which was a very speedy snake) would race across the lower extremity of the rattler and the rattler would strike—but after the snake had passed over his body. Instead of poisoning the snake, he would succeed only in striking himself, thus taking his own life with his own poison. This is what hatred does to the very soul of the hater.

Hate also wills the nonexistence of another human being. It is not the same as willing the destruction of another person; such is often the aim of bitterness and hostility. Hate is at another and a more profound level; it undermines the very being of the other by affirming his nonexistence and accepting this affirmation as true and authentic. It is a withdrawal of sanction of the other as existing. The person is not destroyed, for this would be to acknowledge

45

his existence, but it is to say that he is not there. Of course this is a delusion, but it may be extremely functional in behavior. This is refined evil.

●

There is still another way by which those behind the wall may deal with the anatomy of their predicament. They may recognize the wall for what it is and for the general attitude that it inspires. That is to say, the wall surrounds the Negro wherever he happens to be. When he is out of the segregated area as such, it matters little because it is a part of his person as seen by white society. In 1960, when I was in Bangkok, Mrs. Thurman and I had scheduled ourselves for a boat tour of the river. We were called for at our hotel by the tour guide. When we reached the pier, there were two other persons seated in the boat. As soon as they saw us, the man took the guide aside to say that he and his wife would have to cancel the trip because they could not ride in the same boat with "those people."

During World War I, a second cousin was a YMCA overseas secretary. He served with soldiers at a rest center behind the lines. The men liked him very much because he was both genial and helpful—which was a way he had. One day a company of soldiers came in en route to the front. As was his custom, he greeted each man with an extended hand. When he came to one of the soldiers, he was temporarily stunned by the man's attitude. "No sir," the soldier said, "I don't shake hands with niggers at home or abroad."

Such is a device of control which is manipulated by men who are afraid but who may not recognize their fear as fear. Despite this

46

lack of awareness they seem to be totally captured by their fear. The segregated persons, in this instance the Negroes, who are aware of the fear, may put forth genuine effort to help white persons to see their behavior for what it is and what it is doing to them, their children, and the total world of their values. All available resources must be brought to bear to release them from their enforced bondage. Of such is a crucial part of the redemptive work of nonviolent direct action. In a previous book* on spiritual disciplines I have written an analysis of nonviolence and will not detail it here.

The issue at stake is to find a way by which fear is abandoned and men are free to act responsibly as citizens in the first instance and as citizens committed to values that are moral and ethical in the second instance. It is true that fear in the lives of the disadvantaged exposes them to be controlled by the advantaged. For generations fear has been the monitor, the angel with the flaming sword standing guard to make the pattern of segregation effective. I am concerned at this point with the fear that well-nigh absolute power inspires in the lives of people against whom the power is exercised. Such fear is the survival response to, or technique for, managing life so as to reduce the radical exposure to violence or the threat of violence. The simplest way to do this is to restrict one's life to operate within the confined area of segregation. We have seen how this works. Fear is spawned and kept alive by the perpetual threat of violence everywhere, on all sides. It is violence under unique circumstances and conditions. It is one-sided, uneven violence; it is violence that is devoid of contest. If two men equally motivated, or relatively matched, are in deadly combat, the violence

* *Disciplines of the Spirit* (New York: Harper & Row, 1963).

is clear cut though terrible; there is gross equality of advantage. But when the power and the tools of violence are all on one side, the fact that there is no available and recognized protection from violence makes the resulting fear deeply terrifying.

Until very recently in the South, white persons—by virtue of economic, social, religious, and political power—had dead-weight advantages over Negroes who were essentially without that kind of power. The sufferers knew that they could not fight back effectively, they could not protect themselves, and that in the name of law and order or religion, they could not expect protection from their persecutors. Any slight conflict, any alleged insult, any vague whim, any unrelated frustration, would bring down upon the head of the defenseless the full weight of naked physical violence. Even in such a circumstance it was not the fear of death that was most often at work; it was the deep humiliation arising from dying without cause or purpose. No high end was served. There was no trumpet blast to stir the blood and to anesthetize the agony. There was no going down to the grave with a shout; it was merely being killed or being beaten in utter wrath or indifferent sadism, without the dignity of being on the receiving end of a premeditated act hammered out in the white heat of a transcendent moral passion. The whole experience attacked the fundamental sense of self-respect and personal dignity without which a man is a no-man.

●

Of course all through the years there have been many instances in which Negroes acted against segregation, transcending the fear, or in whom the fear was conspicuously absent. But this whole picture is undergoing a startling change. There are several factors that have operated to release Negroes from the fear of reprisal for rejecting segregation. One such element is the worldwide stirring of subject peoples. It is a phenomenon that seems to me to be the winds of God blowing across the planet. As far back as 1935, when I was in India, there was a noticeable current of freedom stirring in the air. One day in Calcutta, Mrs. Thurman and I were seated in our compartment on the train en route to Santiniketan. Just before the train pulled out, a British officer of the Indian army entered the compartment. Behind him was a terribly emaciated Indian porter carrying two large metal cases. He placed them in the baggage rack. The officer gave him a very small coin—it may have been a penny. Whereupon the porter spat on the floor, and looked into the officer's face as he threw the coin out of the window. The total movement was done to the accompaniment of an angry outburst. The officer reacted promptly by striking the porter across the face with his bamboo swagger stick. The porter snatched it out of his hand, broke it on his spindly kneecap, and threw it out of the window as the train was slowly moving out of the station. Then he ran along the outside of the carriage, hurling insults until he was outdistanced. For the next hour the officer sat in a quiet rage, muttering to himself, and saying among other things in his monologue, "It's time for all decent Englishmen to leave this country when a ———— coolie would dare to insult a British sahib. I am going to retire. Yes, it's time."

Such incidents could be duplicated in many parts of the world. The change in the mobility of colored peoples made the walls of segregation less and less tenable. This change has been precipitated by two world wars and the scattering of colored troops in lands far

49

removed from the places of their birth and upbringing. Particularly has this been true of the American Negro. It was not an accident that in the period following World War I, this country was swept by active racial conflict and angry violence. And the basis of this conflict: men who returned from the wars were unwilling to settle once again behind the segregated walls. They rejected the pattern. And importantly, the threat of violence or the implementation of violence was no longer a deterrent to hold them within the zones of agreement as defined by the pattern. They were used to violence in defense of country and a new stake in the country became evident.

Meanwhile, the country itself was undergoing change. This change was more dramatic and noticeable during and after World War II. The enemy of the united or democratic nations was defined as fascist. The leader of the movement was Adolf Hitler. Fascism as expressed in this man's leadership had at its core a hard metaphysical purpose. It was a social and political order. Its goals were definite and definitive. It delineated the new order in clear terms. It defined man and undertook to determine by certain orders who was worthy to belong and who was not. Against this the democracies, so-called, could not do less than match a definite order from within their own concepts with the definite order of fascism. In other words, democracy had to be defined, given specific content, and a formal declaration of its intent and program had to be voiced. A slogan such as "Make the world safe for democracy" had no standing in such a context. The demand was for concretion, not abstraction. The more definite became the content of the democratic dogma on the part of the United States, for example, the more apparent became the denial of democracy within the

50

common life and the body politic. How did democracy work at home? What was the meaning of the Four Freedoms for all people living within the several countries—and for the Negro, particularly, within his own country?

The total effect of this change in the domestic scene was very marked. In the first place, the sense of isolation, of being cut off behind walls of segregation, began slowly to disappear. Whole families moved out of the South to northern, eastern, and western centers of population to work in war industry. It was not an accident that most of the riots of the period took place outside of the South or in border states or cities. The pattern tended to follow the moving population. The pattern became as mobile as the people. But the mobility, with all that went with it, tended to shake the fears that made control behind the pattern effective. More and more the feeling emerged that Negroes were no longer alone.

Advances in communication play an important role also, until at last any incident can be reported all over the country, or the world for that matter. It came to me with a start, the subtle change that had come over me increasingly in the last decade because of the difference in communication. As a boy and a young man, I lived with the sense that no one would know if I became the victim of violence—I mean no one beyond the tight circle of those behind the wall. But now it could very easily be on the front page of the newspapers of the world in a few hours if there was a disposition so to do, or on worldwide television and radio, for that matter. This makes for an enormous difference in the inside feel of one's emotions.

In the second place, the awareness of segregation and its total effect on the lives of all people caught in its pattern has grown immeasurably all over the country. The sense of responsibility as well as of guilt has increased and it is no longer confined to a single area. Most dramatic has been the world image of America as the leader of the free nations. What we see operating here is an enlarged dimension of the same situation growing out of the announcement of the Four Freedoms during the war. In order to have integrity in its moral leadership, America has been forced to admit the evils of segregation before the whole world and to try to be convincing in its claim that it is seeking to abolish it. There is real spiritual growth in admitting that one's life is not blameless even as one is dedicated effectively to working for the blameless life. And this has been good. In a sense it is a tribute to the moral stature of a country for people beyond its borders to insist that its behavior is unworthy of its profession.

This line of thinking was brought to the center of focus in my mind when President Kennedy was assassinated. At the time I was lecturing at the University of Ibadan in Nigeria, West Africa. I copy these words from my journal written at the time:

"Was his assassination something deep in the psyche of America that rejected its moral leadership in the world? Was it a symbol of the extent to which that leadership has been betrayed? And is all that has come up out of the bowels of the American people some deep awareness that we cannot escape our destiny? I wonder. I am sure that we did not realize before how his symbol of our destiny as a nation in the world had given hope and courage to millions around the world. I do not mean because of foreign aid or loans or anything quite materialistic, but rather a sense of collective American responsibility to Life because of the grace that has made America what it is. Even when we were maligned and cursed because we did not give enough or because we were money mad or proud or bigoted, this was the world's way of saying, 'To whom much is given, much is required—it is the law of life—it is the destiny of men and nations.' Somehow there was a universal feeling that Kennedy knew this and understood it with his heart, and his youth made it authentic in a way that would not have been true had he been full of years and the wisdom that often goes with years. In him it seemed as if the conscience, the informed conscience, of the country was articulate. For a moment in time he seemed the voice of that conscience. It may be that what all kinds of people are feeling is that each must *be* that conscience where he is living and functioning in his private world of being."

●

One further comment is in order about the impact of World War II in particular on the fears that controlled and held back the people behind the walls. I refer to the rise of the Japanese and the galvanic effect that it had on the nonwhite peoples of the world. I do not wish to be misunderstood here. The conquests of the Japanese, short-lived as they were, marked the first time in modern history when the presumptive right of white people to dominate and control nonwhite peoples was effectively challenged. I am not making a case for war in general or for the attack of the Japanese on Pearl Harbor—far from it. What I am saying is that the control of white power over most of the earth was challenged by nonwhite power. This, I am convinced, was merely incidental, but the secondary or concomitant results were far-reaching. I am not even suggesting that this was a war aim of the Japanese. I do not know and as far as I am concerned, it is irrelevant. The point is that given the Japanese attacks and temporary conquests in the Pacific, there flowed from this an awareness that the power that controlled so much of the total life of nonwhite peoples all over the world was not invincible. They were men, just ordinary men, and their power was incidental to their color. It marked the beginning of the end of a certain kind of imperialism and made the whole issue of captive peoples negotiable. There were many other factors at work, but for my purposes this element is crucial.

With the rise of the African nations, a new kind of hope began to stir deep behind the segregated walls. It cannot be measured—the effect of seeing African statesmen in the United Nations and hearing and seeing them on radio and television. A whole new something was in the land, and within the shadow of the walls, there were strange and wonderful stirrings.

The awareness of segregation has been greatly augmented by the increase in communication. This is important and crucial. The total planetary atmosphere has become sensitive and it is now literally true that "no man is an island, no man stands alone." What at one time was the sheer insight of the poet, the prophet, the spiritual genius, has now become literal fact. The deep desolation created by the sense of isolation has been displaced by the sure knowledge that eyes are everywhere; soon or late and sooner than later what is done in a weary Mississippi swamp or in a dark Harlem alley will find its way before the television camera and broadcaster's booth. This is not to imply that all is known and all is being revealed. There still remains the anonymity of sadism and brutality moving through the nighttime and haunting the lonely jail cell and the back country road and the dimly lighted city street. But the word is abroad.

54

This new and widely spread awareness undermines the fear of violence. When a man knows that what he may suffer can be and will be shared vicariously by many others, this gives to him a strange new courage. He enters into a fellowship of sufferers and he does not seem to himself to be alone. The degree to which his suffering is shared by others marks the potential that such suffering may itself become redemptive. But this is to introduce a sophisticated notion which the sufferer himself may not have. What he does have is the strength that comes to him from the knowledge that his cry will be heard and his agony felt beyond the pain in his own body and the hurt of his own spirit.

It is important, therefore, that there be the kind of activity that will bring out into the open the hidden springs of prejudice that are obscured by accepted social norms and patterns of cultural behavior expressed in statutes and custom. A way of life in the South and to a lesser extent in the North has so settled itself in the common life that the fact that such a way of life is predicated upon the segregation of Negroes is a part of the landscape. It is taken for granted; the rightness of it is not a matter of challenge but rather it is a gross collective assumption. Any person who questions the grounds of the society, who raises a primary question of human values, is in truth a disturber of the peace and a troublemaker. Such an accusation is entirely correct. Most often men do not want to seem to be troublemakers. Rauschenbusch used to tell his students that there are many good people in the world but there are a very few who are good enough to disturb the devil.

The waters must be troubled. In fine, all of the events discussed in this section have the net effect of troubling the waters. But nothing must be taken for granted here. Individuals themselves must trouble the waters. This is one of the important contributions that is made by the demonstrations. The more peaceful the demonstrations, the more they are apt to trouble the waters. This is true because the hostility that the demonstration may inspire cannot be focused on angry or violent behavior. The demonstration has to be focused on the evil itself or the exposure of the states of mind out of which retaliation may spring; men see themselves pouring out their venom on those who refrain *deliberately* from retaliation. Of course, this assumes a basic decency and humaneness which may be gratuitous. I do not know. Here again, the fact of widespread publicity in pictures, television, and radio makes it possible for a man, his family, and his friends to see him as he performs his defensively and offensively vicious acts. What father is there who can give a satisfactory answer to his daughter when she sees him striking a girl her age with a club or knocking her down with a stream of water from a fire hose? Suppose she asks him why he did it? All the stock replies would be given and these perhaps would satisfy her. But even though she understood what he was saying and accepted it without question because it fitted into all that she had been taught to believe about Negroes, she may sense another meaning. There is the real possibility that despite the pride which he feels and expresses as a defender of white supremacy, there is conceivably, even for him, a deeper issue here. There is something in human life that moves far beneath the surface of conventions by which a particular life is given meaning, which makes a man shrink from being stripped of all feelings of mercy and compassion. Thus stripped to the literal element of personality, even such a man may be unwilling to relax his hold, however fragmentary, upon his claim to call himself a human being. Thus once again the increase in communication helps create a conscience against, and an awareness of, the evil of segregation and its off-springs. It makes segregation and racial prejudice a matter of discussion and examination.

Thus, the third alternative for those who are segregated is within reach of all who seek it. The wall can be recognized for what it is—a wall. After that, the sufferers can put forth every effort to bring home to the offenders the true meaning of the thing which they are perpetuating and the evilness of the evil situation can stand clear on the horizon of the common life. This cannot be accomplished until and unless Negroes are shed of their fear. The fear is not of the white man as such, but it is the fear of the *threat* of violence which he is free to project, remorselessly, if he chooses. With this fear cast off, Negroes at last will be free just to be citizens, members of the society—good citizens, bad citizens, indifferent citizens, but citizens.

●

I have spoken of what the overall change in world climate in general and the American climate in particular contributes to the loss of fear. But there is something more. One may lose fear also by a sense of being a part of a company of people who share the same concerns and are conscious of participating in the same collective destiny. This is an additional form that the feeling of community inspires. A strange and wonderful courage often comes into a man's life when he shares a commitment to something that is more important than whether he himself lives or dies. It is the discovery of the dynamic character of life itself. This may not be a conscious act as far as the rationale for it is concerneed. It *is* a

57

discovery of the conditions under which fresh resources of energy are available. When a person is able to place at the disposal of a single end, goal, or purpose the resources of his life, his strength is magnified a hundredfold or even a thousandfold. He relaxes his hold upon his own physical existence because he is caught up in the kind of enlarged consciousness or expanded awareness that is triggered by the commitment that his life becomes important only in terms that fulfill the inscrutable demands of the commitment. Such an experience is spiritual; yea, it is religious. In such a moment a man has the feeling that he is totally encompassed, totally alive, and more completely himself than he has ever been before. Under such a circumstance, even death is a little thing. This is the reason why there is a kind of fervor—not hysteria but a kind of fervor—that so often illumines the countenances of those who are peacefully demonstrating in the face of the threat of violence. I recognize that there may be mass hysteria into which people are caught up and the ability to stick by one's witness under duress may be created out of hostility and an overriding anger. But there is another and vaster possibility which has made itself manifest here and there during these fateful days: a deep spiritual awareness that one's life is in vital touch with the Source of Being that holds and makes secure against all that destroys and lays waste.

Black chauvinism may produce the same intensity of courage. It may create a fresh, new sense of being born again to take up arms and fight even though one knows at the time that victory is impossible; one may win a skirmish here and there but the war is lost even before it begins. But in the heat of battle, in that fierce unswerving sense of standing one's ground, not giving way either in the name of love, hate, country, or religion, there is a moment when all the bells ring and one goes down to the grave with a shout. The appeal of this chauvinism cannot be lightly dismissed. Its weakness lies in the fact that it is the way of reward and punishment, the way of retribution and vengeance. It is one more turn of the same wheel that moves round and round but does not gain an inch. Such fierceness of manner and deed plants the seeds of ill will and bitterness which will bear the same kind of fruit for one's children and one's children's children. It is a denial of the possibility of a good and bountiful future. It says that the contradictions of life are not only final but ultimate. It is a vote against life. Surely it confirms men in their hostility and hardens the heart. Despite this, there is something very compelling about the persuasive quality of inspiration that flows from courageous men fighting and losing against great and overwhelming odds. But when the battles are over, Negroes and white people must live together in the United States. To forget this is the great betrayal of the future.

●

How may the white person deal with segregation? In the first place, he may accept the fact and the station. This is too obvious for comment because it is the general attitude. Yet it is worthy of some analysis. As we have seen, segregation is accepted and it has had a general consensus for a long time. It is apart from my purpose, even if I were competent so to do, to discuss the origin and the history of the pattern of segregation. The facile acceptance of the pattern of segregation is rooted in certain aspects of the culture. The identification of blackness with evil, with the ominous, the destructive, the terrifying, is all through the language both sacred and profane. Black magic is evil; so is a black crime, but a white lie is acceptable. One could go on.

In a religion such as Christianity, the image of God in the mind of many Christians is that of a kindly, benevolent, bewiskered white man, seated on a white throne, surrounded by blond and brunette angels who stand ready to serve Him in praises or as messengers. The Devil, on the other hand, is the Prince of Darkness while the imps of the Devil are black. Hence the phrase "black as an imp." Now this is strong medicine even for the pure in heart. What a vote of confidence it must have been to a white person to feel that the Creator of the Universe was made in his image. Of course, there is nothing unusual about the notion that God is imaged in accordance with the ideal of the beholder. The advantage is obvious.

One of the things most puzzling to Gandhi about slavery was the fact that the slaves accepted the religion of the masters. This meant that the psychological and moral advantage was always on the side of the slave system. Slave and master prayed to the same God—but as slave and master. Gandhi wondered why the slaves did not become Muslims. It was a sheer speculation but in theory it was a sound idea, for, as he took pains to point out, the religion of Mohammed is the only world religion that does not practice discrimination within the faith itself. In the presence of Allah there is neither rich or poor, wise or foolish, black or white, brown or yellow—but all are one before Him. This means encompassing all diversity and all differences.

When I was working as a summer director of religious education in a church in Roanoke, Virginia, during the mid-twenties, I came into the young people's meeting one Sunday evening and discovered that a stranger was addressing the group. It developed that he was from the west coast of Africa. He was saying to the group that he had come into the city en route to West Virginia and found that he had a few hours' wait between trains. Continuing, he said, "Since it was the Christian Sabbath, I decided to visit a church. The first church I found was on the other end of the street. When I entered I was told that I was at the wrong church. This was the First Baptist Church white and what I wanted was the First Baptist Church colored."

Then with deep stirring of emotion he said, "Allah laughs aloud in His Muslim Heaven when He beholds the Christian spectacle: First Baptist Church colored! First Baptist Church white!" The fact that the Muslim faith recognizes no barriers separating the believers is one of its most challenging appeals.

The consensus for segregation goes even deeper than cultural images reflected in the imaginative lore of the dominant religion. For instance, in Christianity the interpretation of the doctrine of salvation by grace has had no small part in lending support to the arrogance and pride of race. Bear in mind that the point under discussion is what happens when white America accepts the status of segregation and when the basis of segregation is given a general consensus.

For more than a hundred years Christianity has had the missionary enterprise as a part of its fundamental undertaking. The mission study program has been an integral part of religious training and education. In systematic plan the various peoples of the earth have been studied and serviced. Year after year throughout the Christian movement there have been courses on the African peoples, India, Burma, Latin America, American Negroes, American Indians, etc. Such courses are replete with statistical data, human interest stories, tales of heroism, intimate studies of the lives of individual "natives" who have been converted, etc. And all of this has had high motivation and has tended to stir the conscience of people to the end that money, goods, and even the lives of people as well as their skills shall be given freely and redemptively. All of this has been and continues to be good for what it does and is. And what is that? It is and continues to be an effort to identify with the needs of others and to administer to those needs effectively. The basic aim, of course, is to take the Gospel of Jesus Christ to the world, to save men's souls for Christ. This doctrine of salvation demands that all men everywhere should know Jesus Christ as Savior. In essence, however, there is something else that is an essential ingredient in the doctrine: salvation whenever and wherever it occurs is an expression of God's grace.

Let us examine this carefully. Salvation is the work of grace made possible through the life, death, suffering, and resurrection of Jesus Christ, the Redeemer. Initially, then, salvation comes as the wind, to use a gospel image of the coming of the Kingdom. There is no merit. Those who carried the message at home or abroad felt, yea *knew,* that they had received God's grace quite without merit, which is the way grace manifests itself. Those who were without the message had not been so favored.

The curious distortion given to this by the Ku Klux Klan and various Christian Front organizations is to be understood by anyone who takes the time to read the literature. The argument for slavery has some of its basis here. It goes further to insist that in comparison with being brought to a Christian country that they

62

may be in the "Way" of salvation, the rigors of slavery are a little thing. Now, the gift of God—grace—is one of the central facets of the faith; it is also a part of the Divine Mystery. If all are in the "Way" of grace and one man receives and another does not, who knows but that the man who does not receive it may have his will to resist stiffened by an act of God. The idea that God, for hidden reasons, may influence the spirit of man against Him is not unknown to readers of the Bible. But be that as it may. If one man has salvation and another does not, it would follow quite easily that God in His wisdom has His own inscrutable reason for this simple but terrible discrimination. He must be deeply aware of something, some undisclosed flaw, that is hidden from mortal knowledge and judgment. If such is my thought that I, through no obvious merit on my part, am conscious of my salvation, even as I am conscious of your lack of salvation, then it just may be that God does see something in me that calls forth His redeeming love (the doctrine of grace to the contrary) that He does not see in you. Such a notion is not hard to come by. I knew a man many years ago who had a quaint reply always to the question, "Well, how are you today?" "If God Almighty has any favorite children, I am one of them," was the reply.

If God sees aught in me that is better, more worthy, more meritorious than what He sees in you, then it is inescapable that I would feel that in the nature of the case, I am somehow better than you are. If I am better, I am therefore superior. My conscious experience of grace may make this manifest. It is but a breath and a whisper to the whole sordid and baleful insinuation of racial, class, and religious arrogance and the sprawling notions of superiority. It is unspeakably ironical that the tremendous doctrine

63

of grace may become a part of the supporting ground for racial and religious bigotry. Thus a man may carry the Gospel to an "outsider" with the hope and the fervent prayer that he may be helped into the way of grace and salvation. To that end he may sacrifice his substance, his status, even his life because his identification with the outsider's need is so demanding. Always, then, such a man can identify with the other's needs, predicament, and context without ever identifying with the man himself. The whole world can be saved, redeemed, and at the same time, the true relation between the giver and the receiver remain untouched, uninfluenced. To be specific: because a man is a Christian is no indication to me what his attitude may be toward me in any given circumstance.

It is not to be understood that the evangelical and the missionary impact tends to have no influence on the true relationship between people as people. It is to be understood that the curious distortion or corruption of the doctrine of grace supports a social attitude that is completely foreign to the mood and the spirit of the doctrine itself. Consequently, it is entirely possible that I, for instance, can work for the redemption of the souls of people, help them in their need in many critical ways, while at the same time keep them out of my neighborhood, out of my school, and out of my local church. And all of this with no apparent conflict in values or disturbance of conscience.

When a white person accepts the fact and the status of segregation he can carry on the normal intercourse of his life without being aware of it. In many superficial ways he may remain unaffected by it. He can live his entire life in a thousand communities all over the country and have no primary contact with Negroes. He can be secure in his own feeling of superiority, unchallenged.

64

Or, as has been suggested, he can exercise his good will within the limitations vouched safe to him by his acceptance of the white person's status within the accepted pattern. But whether the acceptance is deliberate or indifferent, he becomes the party to a monstrous evil executed in his name and maintained in his behalf. The responsibility for the social decay and defiling of the spirit is inescapable, acknowledged or unacknowledged. For segregation is a sickness and no one who lives in its reach can claim or expect immunity. It makes men dishonest by forcing them to call an evil thing good; it makes them discourteous and rude when it is contrary to their temperaments and sense of values to be so. I received a copy of a letter sent from a ticket agent in a Southern community to the chaplain of a nearby Negro college. The letter bore no greeting. The agent could not even use the conventional word "Dear" in formal salutation.

●

A second attitude of a white person toward segregation may be a resentful helplessness, with anger or angry violence, or with guilt. The rationalization for what I am calling resentful helplessness runs somewhat as follows. Segregation is the accepted pattern of the American way of life. It is the one sure way to keep the Negro from being completely eliminated in the unequal struggle for survival in our society. It tailor-makes his environment to suit and to meet his peculiar needs. By temperament, background, character, and ability he is different from the white person and therefore he has to be dealt with in a special manner. In his separate educational facilities, he can be taught the things that are within his potential to grasp and understand. He does not need the same kind of training given to the rest of us because he will be living and working among his own people. If he is given the same training alongside us, he would be unfit for the life that he must live as a Negro among Negro people. After all, he is not white . . . so the arguments run.

At the beginning of my senior year at Morehouse College, in the fall of 1922, I applied to the Newton Theological Seminary in Massachusetts for admission to study for the ministry. My application was rejected because at that time this particular seminary did not admit Negroes as students. In the letter which was sent to me, it was suggested that I should seek entrance to Virginia Union University (a Negro institution) where I could be trained in the kind of leadership that I would need in order to serve my own people.

The notion is that the Negro is happiest among his own people. A Negro belong with Negroes. After all, an individual who seeks to underscore his helplessness may say that he did not create the pattern. He would not know how to change it if he could. Besides, we have as much as we can handle with our own undesirable white people. There is a natural resistance in being disturbed by having the moral question raised about segregation. But always there is the sneaking rumor that will not be silenced: all is not well behind the walls. It may be the chance acquaintance with a Negro who pulls aside the curtain of the countenance and recalls a true view of the inner landscape. It is then that the other person discovers a whole new world of meaning of which he was not aware before. It may be a story on television, a newscast about people from some other part of the world, a play or a novel, perhaps an interview of a statesman from the United Nations in which he recalls how he may have been treated at a roadside restaurant. Something suddenly stabs the conscience awake and a whole new dimension of one's commonplace life is brought directly into focus.

Often such awakening catapults one on the defensive. The most common remark is that the true picture is not understood. For instance, apologists say that the South is the best and most congenial place for the Negro. Further, it is said that the Southern white person understands him thoroughly, he knows how to deal with him; there is a bond between them that holds against all ruptures and violences. It is amazing how widespread such a notion is. Many persons from some other part of the country defer to the man from the South if the Negro has to be dealt with or directed. The general statement is that the Southerner understands the psychology of the Negro, etc. Times without number in my experiences as a preacher and lecturer all over the country and beyond, I have encountered persons from the South who, strangers though they were, presumed to cast themselves in a role of utter familiarity by word, manner, and deed. Their attitude seemed to say, "We have a secret, you and I. We won't tell."

The South has inherited from the past a deep inferiority feeling. There is some ground for this, to be sure. For a long time it was and continues to be the most impoverished region of the country. It has not recovered from the ravages of the Civil War and an economy built upon conscript and slave labor and King Cotton. It has been made to feel deeply ashamed and guilty because of slavery and its side effects. It has been forced to find its significances in the myths and delusions of a past grandeur, causing it to back into the future with its attention riveted on yesterday. The

67

result is that the South's attitude toward the rest of the country is belligerent and angry. The most dramatic occasion for this, if not the cause, revolves around the Negro. The basic issue involving the Negro, in turn, is segregation and its social significance. It is for this reason that the South has a Cause and its Cause was yesterday. It is not a lost Cause; it is simply outdated. And the symbol of that Cause is the Negro.

Wherever such a white person from the South goes, he carries his Cause with him. The result of this kind of behavior is to make the Cause current wherever he goes. The only way that this can be accomplished is to center it around a living human being who in his person and his very existence updates the Cause. It is the very intensity of his effort to keep his Cause current that gives to his attitude a kind of contagion. Some years ago I boarded the last coach of an Illinois Central train en route from Chicago to Memphis. It happened that I sat in a seat directly opposite a lady who sat alone with her suitcases. It was obvious from her facial expression that she was alarmed by my presence. When the conductor came through for tickets, he reached my seat first. After taking my ticket, he turned to receive hers, whereupon she asked him, "What is *that* doing in this car?" pointing toward me. The conductor said, "*That* has a ticket." There followed a very astounding performance. She visited for a few minutes with each of ten people who was seated alone. In unmistakeable tones, she told each one about what was allowed and not allowed in Mississippi where she came from. Slowly the attitude of the entire coach changed toward my presence. It was a visible transformation from indifference and a general casualness to sensitivity and in one instance at least to hostility.

Yet it must be remembered, as was pointed out earlier, that in the South the Negro counts. This is a fact that is not often considered. His presence is never ignored; indeed it cannot easily be ignored. Into the very warp and woof of the life of the South his very substance is woven. All of this is to say that it was important for the South and its Cause that the Negro be counted into the total scheme, but on the terms of the white power structure. Great care had to be exercised that the Negro must not seem to himself to count. For if in his own estimation he counted, then this would render him increasingly useless to the Cause of the South. The degree to which he counted to himself, to that degree would his very presence be a threat to the whole order of the region. This is a very crucial but subtle distinction. The Negro must be important to the very fabric of the region, as the living symbol of the Cause of the South, but care must be exercised that he must not so regard himself. Always he must be a silent partner, an unselfconscious pawn in the hands of Southern necessity. The Negro had to be available to the South but his importance must not be a part of his estimate of his own significance either to himself or to the South. What a difference it would have made in the whole story of the South had the Negro been permitted to be an active partner in the development and growth of the South.

Once in Mexico City I stood at the base of one of the ancient Aztec Pyramids while a guide was recounting the story of the famed Empire. He said that the Aztecs had conquered all the kingdoms around only to discover that such military conquests had placed the whole structure of their religion in jeopardy. At a certain time each year the most important rite in their religious ceremony was the sacrificing of a young healthy male warrior who

69

had been taken in battle. He was sacrificed at the top of the pyramid and his body hurled down the steps before the assembly at the base. But when all the surrounding nations were conquered, there were no sacrifices available. Very thoughtfully it was decided to "unconquer" a nation, engage it in battle once a year, capture a healthy young man and sacrifice him at the appointed time. The nation's importance was its availability for an enterprise that was dependent upon it but concerning which it had no responsible decisions to make. It was the silent partner, involved but not personally committed.

Segregation is the status that keeps a group available for sacrifice and thus keeps the cult of the South intact and in health. Hence when it is threatened, the fear, the anger, and the guilt become manifest. Any attack on the system is an attack on the world of meaning and reality of the South. Every defense, even to the taxing of all the total resources, must be rallied. It is not so much a fight against Negroes as such, as it is a fight in defense of the soul of the region, of the religion of the cult. And this is the measure of the estimate that the South places upon the significance of the life of the Negro in its midst. It is only in latter days of desperation that one hears spokesmen express a willingness for Negroes to leave the region.

As paradoxical as it may seem, here we see the work of a profound truism in human relations. The measure of one man's estimate of another is often found in the power of the kind of weapon that he feels he must use in order to contain him. When our children were very small and I accompanied them on visits to their grandmothers in Florida and in Arkansas, it was necessary again and again to help them deal with the deep hurt and pain of segregation. "Why can't we go over there and swing in the playground?" "Why can't we go in there and get a dish of ice cream?" "Why must we sit in this crowded coach and there is plenty of room in the other coach?" "Why must we sit in this dirty railway waiting room and the other waiting room is so clean and well-lighted?"

With great care and in as resourceful a manner as my love and imagination could conjure, I tried to make it clear to them that the measure of a man's estimate of you is the extent to which he feels he must go in order to hold you in a designated place. I would say to them that segregation indicates the extent to which men may go to isolate themselves from others and it therefore is an expression of their estimation of the strength of the isolated ones. A white society must array all the forces of legislation and law enforcement: it must falsify the facts of history, tamper with the insights of religion and religious doctrine, editorialize and slant news and the printed word. On top of that it must keep separate schools, separate churches, separate graveyards, and separate public accommodations—all this in order to freeze the place of the Negro in society and guarantee his basic immobility. Yet all this is but partial indication of the high estimate that such a society places upon him. Once again, to state it categorically: The measure of a man's estimate of your strength is the kind of weapons he feels that he must use in order to hold you fast in a prescribed place.

A single but classic illustration of the whole notion is to be found in the biblical account of David and Goliath. Goliath, as he faced David, indicated by his appearance what was his estimate of David. He wore his battle armor, including breastplate, visor, short and long sword. And David? He was dressed in a single simple tunic. And his weapon? It was a slingshot! That was his estimate of Goliath's strength. It may be that the shock gave Goliath a stroke; and it was all over.

The form or the manifestation of this high regard or estimate is fear! It is not the fear of the strange and unfamiliar, but it is the fear of retribution and vengeance. There is a deep center of anxiety within white society that is created and sustained by an abiding sense of collective guilt, but held in place by the inverted notion of the strength and power of the Negro. It is the ancient fear which the strong have of the weak. This is aptly illustrated in an account found in T. R. Glover's *The Influence of Christ in the Ancient World*. He quotes the précis of a letter of Pliny and the Emperor Trajan's reply.

Pliny to Trajan:

When I was absent in another part of the province, Nicomedeia was visited with a serious fire, which destroyed many private houses and two public buildings, the Gerusia and the temple of Isis. The fire spread, both owing to the wind and the lethargy of the people, who are said to have remained mere spectators of the disaster. And indeed there are no fire-engines or buckets, and no appliances for extinguishing fires. I have given orders for these to be provided. It is for you to decide whether a *collegium* of firemen should not be formed, not to exceed 150 in number. I will take care that they are bona fide firemen, and that their privileges are not used for other purposes. It cannot be hard to watch so small a number.

Trajan to Pliny:

You think that a society (*collegium*) of firemen might be formed at Nicomedeia, as at many other places. But we must re-

72

member that your province has been especially disturbed by factions arising from such institutions. Whatever name they bear, it is almost certain that men so united will become a political club. It will be better therefore to supply the necessary apparatus in case of fire, to warn the landlords to take precautions for themselves, and, in case of necessity, to make use of the populace in extinguishing fires.*

There is a mystery that surrounds the injured and suppressed. It is impossible to get a clear reading of what is going on. "What are they thinking about?" "What is going on behind the high walls of segregation?" "What do the eyes of the injured say when they look into the face of the injurer?"

It was in an effort to probe the mystery, or at least to create a screen to hide it, that the image of the Negro as a buffoon and clown has been perpetuated. During the period of slavery, it must have been a consolation and reassurance, in the uneasy times for the slave master and friends, to be entertained by the dancing and clowning of some articulate slaves. It was easy for him to delude himself into thinking that only a happy and contented man could be so freely creative in his buffoonery. Such slaves were rewarded by occasional preferential treatment. They became the instruments of the dream of the happy slave. Such a notion was further aided by the singing and the manner of the slave when he was meeting his own personal needs of pleasure and worship. The point need not be labored; it is merely to suggest that the image of the Negro as an entertaining fool served the important purpose of supplying content and meaning to the mystery surrounding the life of the injured, the hurt, the oppressed. It is to be noted that this illusion has still some currency.

* New Haven: Yale University Press, 1929, pp. 30-31.

73

It was and continues to be the silence that is ominous and threatening. Mark Twain gives the account from his childhood concerning the slave boy with whom he grew up. Whenever the slave boy sang or whistled, Mark Twain's mother said she felt comforted and secure. But when he was silent, as he would be sometimes, then she became anxious and nervous.

●

This high estimate takes another inverted form: white society tends to demand more of a Negro than it demands of a white person in the same situation. It is not only because there may be an effort to eliminate the Negro by such high demand or standards. It is not merely to keep him out of competition and thus guarantee his limited or inferior status. But there is something else quietly at work here. This high demand, the nearly impossible odds, say that there is a superior person here and his ability ought to make possible a much more than average performance. Such an interpretation can very easily be regarded as a form of rationalization. As indeed it is. The mind has to make sense of its experience with the world. What I am saying is that every effort that is made to eliminate the Negro person by the excessive demand says also that those who behave in that manner are revealing a hidden element in their attitude—the element which indicates that somewhere within the quiet places of their spirit there is a staggering respect for the ability and the power of the Negro. And this is the point. John Steinbeck makes essentially the same observation.

I am constantly amazed at the qualities we expect in Negroes. No race has ever offered another such high regard. We expect

Negroes to be wiser than we are, more tolerant than we are, braver, more dignified than we, more self-controlled and self-disciplined. We even demand more talent from them than from ourselves. A Negro must be ten times as gifted as a white to receive equal recognition. We expect Negroes to have more endurance than we in athletics, more courage in defeat, more rhythm and versatility in music and dancing, more controlled emotion in theatre. We expect them to obey rules of conduct we flout, to be more courteous, more gallant, more proud, more steadfast. In a word, while maintaining that Negroes are inferior to us, by our unquestioning faith in them we prove our conviction that they are superior in many fields, even fields we are presumed to be trained and conditioned in and they are not.

Let me give a few examples.

In the Alabama bus boycott we knew there would be no Negro violence—and there wasn't. The only violence was white violence.

In the streets we expect courtesy from Negroes even when we are ugly and overbearing.

In the prize ring we know a Negro will be game and will not complain at a decision.

In Little Rock we knew that any brutality would originate among the whites.

For a long time whites would not compete against Negroes for fear they might lose. It was said that their coordination—it was called animal coordination—was better and their physical responses quicker.

If there is racial trouble, we are convinced that Negroes will not strike the first blow, will not attack in the night, will not set off bombs, and our belief is borne out by events.

We expect Negroes to be good-tempered and self-controlled under all circumstances.

But our greatest expectation is that they will be honest, honorable, and decent. This is the most profound compliment we can

75

pay any man or group. And the proof of this shows in our outrage when a Negro does not live up to the picture we ordinarily have of him.

With thousands of burglaries, muggings, embezzlements reported every day, we are upset when a Negro is found doing what so many whites do regularly.

In New York, with its daily reports of public thefts, deceits, and assorted political and fiscal raids on public money and treason against public trust, one Negro who succumbs to the temptation to do what many white people do fills us with dismay and the papers are full of it. What greater compliment can we pay to a people?

Finally, let me bring it down to cases.

I have children, as many of you whites who read this have. Do you think your children would have the guts, the dignity, and the responsibility to go to school in Little Rock knowing they would be insulted, shoved, hated, sneered at, even spat upon day after day, and do it quietly without showing anger, petulance, or complaint? And even if they could take it, would they also get good grades?

Now I am a grown, fairly well-educated—I hope intelligent—white man. I know that violence can produce no good effect of any kind. And yet if my child were spat on and insulted, I couldn't trust myself not to get a ball bat and knock out a few brains. But I trust Negroes not to, and they haven't.

I think so much of those school children in Little Rock—a small handful who carry the will and conscience, the hopes and futures of millions in their arms. They have not let their people down. I think, what quiet pride their grandchildren can have in them knowing they came of such stock.

And then I think of the faces of the mob that tried to keep them out, faces drooling hatred, cursing and accursed faces, brave only in numbers, spitting their venom at children. And some of those faces, masked, sneaking in the night to plant a bomb—the final weapon of a coward.

What pride can their descendants take in their ancestry? But of course, they will forget, or lie, or both.

When Martin Luther King was stabbed by a hysterical woman, he might well have felt some anger or hurt or despair. But his first words on coming out of the anesthetic were: "Don't let them hurt her. She needs help."

Perhaps some of the anger against Negroes stems from a profound sense of their superiority, and perhaps their superiority is rooted in having a cause and an unanswerable method composed of courage, restraint, and a sense of direction.*

Of course, the reverse of that operates as well. Here we come upon another of the paradoxes. The relaxed demand, the substandard requirement, seems to be an accommodation to the weakness and inferior quality of the Negro mind or ability. The Grade A Negro college, the man who performs well "for a Negro," what is expected of the Negro must not be equated with what is expected of the white person—these phrases reveal the mood and the notion. For a long time Negro colleges were accredited not as colleges but as Negro colleges. On the one hand, this seems to say that there is an inherent limitation at work and it would be unfair, yes even cruel, not to take such limitation into account in any across-the-board requirement. On the other hand, it may indicate a carefully collective effort to keep certain doors closed and thus freeze the Negro in an inferior status in the total society. Further, it could indicate that there is such a deep unconscious regard for his ability and strength that society cannot dare to run the risk to give him an equal opportunity. If the latter is the point of view of Negroes, then they can make the rejection of the society their strength and a vote of confidence for their ability. All of

* "Atque Vale," *Saturday Review,* July 23, 1960, p. 13. Used by permission.

these considerations are largely spawned by the fear that eats away at the integrity of so-called white society. What a burden this is to carry—what a vast waste of human resources!

●

There is still a third attitude for a white person who undertakes to deal with the fact of segregation: He may recognize it for what it is, a wall that his own insecurity holds in place, and he may seek in all ways possible to remove it. There goes with this initially the true responsibility for exercising the initiative in this matter. Overt power is in the hands of white society. Well within its territory reside the controls. For a long time the yea and the nay have been words belonging uniquely to the vocabulary of white society. But it must be remembered that the old saw that power corrupts and absolute power corrupts absolutely, remains true.

The first point at which the nay or the yea must be said is in the law of the land and in the statutes of the states. Psychologically, this may be beginning at the wrong end. I am not sure. I do not know. But I am convinced that the role of law as a tutor in society cannot be overemphasized. It announces the formal intent of the society and projects on the horizon of the common life a point of referral equally open to all as citizens who fall under its scope and jurisdiction. While I was in India, when it was still a colony of the British Empire, my Indian friends often tried to make clear to me that their position in India was a much happier one than mine as an American Negro. I made clear to them the fact that the limitations under which I suffered were in *violation* of the Constitution of the land and therefore it sat in judgment upon

78

all the civil disabilities from which I suffered. This was for me an enormous basis of hope. True, the Constitution had not spoken directly to my condition, but it would so speak through the due process created by an interpretation of its intent. At that far-off time in the past, the Indian had no such built-in point of referral. Even the right of ownership of his own country was usurped.

Before the law can be heard, it must recover from the loss of prestige and regard from which it has suffered. This loss may be owing to the kind of ruthlessness necessary in the conquest of frontier after frontier in the New World; it may result in part from the violence perpetrated against a moral conscience in the brutalizing and destruction of the American Indian or the like. Whatever may be the cause or causes, there is not a high regard for the law of the land. Of course we are a young adolescent country, which must never be forgotten.

The important aspect of the question involving the law in the matter of the practice of segregation is the general feeling that law is automatically on the side of those who control the power in a society. Thus, law is interpreted and regarded as the theoretical basis of the established pattern of the society. Such an attitude does not make room for justice under law generally but rather does it ignore the demands of justice beyond the interests of the dominant group in the society. It is commonplace that in much of America, law is regarded as a convenience, but this is far from a true picture. There have been throughout our history two basic attitudes toward law. There is the attitude that law is the enemy of the common man primarily because he may be without adequate defense before the law. And yet there are numerous examples of the defenseless being defended and the helpless being protected

79

by a careful interpretation of the law on behalf of the merits of the case.

Among Negroes, particularly in the South and more recently in the North, law has been regarded as a statement against their interest and welfare. The symbol of the law is the policeman. In the South the policeman is most often referred to as "the law." The policeman, the sheriff—these are the representatives of the law; behind them stand the vague items such as statutes and regulations. What the law means is set forth in the behavior and actions of the sheriff and policeman. More often than not, such officers are also white. This means that the creators of the law are white, the interpreters of the law are white, and the enforcers of the law are white. There is little respect for the "majesty of the law," or confidence in the fairness and equality of the law. Add to all this the fact that in the courts themselves the word of a Negro is not the word of a citizen, it is the word of a Negro, and therefore it can never be assessed in the same way that the word of a white man is assessed. This attitude toward law is deeply ingrained. It was so much a part of my own early conditioning that despite the change in my own attitude in this matter, my mind does a double take before I will ask a simple direction of a policeman on the streets of any American city. The felt helplessness of the Negro before the law is notorious.

When I was an undergraduate in the South, a young Negro lawyer gave an address to my senior class about his profession. Among some of the things he told us that day, more than thirty years ago, was the difficulty he had in getting clients when he began his practice. The mood was: it is impossible to get justice even when you have a white lawyer, but if you go into court with a

Negro lawyer before a white judge, white jurors, etc., there was not even the whisper of a chance to be dealt with fairly. Thus in the early days of his practice—or absence of practice—while his mother continued to support him out of income from her hand laundry, he spent all of his time sitting in the courtroom. He was well trained, not only a college graduate but also a graduate of the University of Michigan Law School, and was licensed to practice before all the courts of Georgia and also the U. S. Supreme Court. In fact, he was better trained than many of the white lawyers and even some of the judges. Whenever a Negro was being tried, his silent presence in the courtroom increased the chances for justice immeasurably. The judge and the prosecution and the defense did not want this trained Negro lawyer to see them making a travesty of the law in handling a Negro's case.

Some of the attitudes taken toward decisions of the U. S. Supreme Court further illustrate the contempt for law as expressed in the notion that law is the instrument of defense in the hands of the strong against the weak. Under what conditions do men deliberately go against the law of the land? They may do so by challenging the right of the law-making and law-interpreting bodies to interfere with, and to regulate the full expression of, individual feelings and desires. Such a challenge goes to the foundation of order in society. This does not mean that the individual has no right to make such a challenge, but it does mean that he must do so entirely within the means provided for such challenges through due process of the law. There is an orderly way, a definite procedure which provides for orderly change. But where there is little basic respect for law and order, there is little interest in, nor time for, such procedure. To ignore orderly process is to

81

undermine the structure of a contained society. It is a part of the tradition of our society to resort to measures outside the law when law either breaks down or there is a radical and widespread loss of confidence. In the case of the Negro, there is a long history of the loss of confidence in the law. The fact of his having been at one time a chattel slave under the law is responsible for his lack of confidence in the law and the oftentimes flagrant disregard for the law on the part of white society.

"A slave is in absolute bondage; he has no civil rights," the law maintained. And so a slave could not own property, give or receive gifts, make a will, or inherit property except at his master's pleasure.

More important, the slave could not enter into a contract for any purpose, since "neither his word nor his bond has any standing in law." Hence a slave could not marry: slaves could live together, but their relationship had no legal status. "The relation between slaves," a North Carolina judge wrote, "is essentially different from that of man and wife joined in lawful wedlock . . . for with slaves it may be dissolved at the pleasure of either party, or by the sale of one or both, depending on the caprice or necessity of the owners." Slave law not only refused to recognize marriage, it reversed the common-law tradition that children derive their status from their father, maintaining that "the father of a slave is unknown to our law." To have held otherwise would have raised the embarrassing question of what to do with the numerous children born of a white father and a slave mother; the old common law would thus have created a large class of free mulattoes. Thus a slave father not only was legally unknown, he was legally stripped of the last semblance of masculinity, his right to his marriage bed.*

* "Chattel Law and the Negro" by Charles E. Silberman, *Fortune*, May 1964, p. 166.

Because of this historic attitude, as it is expressed in his minority status today, it is not to be wondered that only in rare instances has the Negro felt able to take the law into his own hands. The rioting in certain Northern cities in 1964 may be interpreted as a measure of the depth of the frustration and futility from which Negroes must suffer to take the law into their own hands and act violently in their own behalf. But such action has been a kind of blind rebellion against unbearable situations rather than a carefully designed flaunting of the law in an effort to force the law to do its work on their behalf as citizens. Here we are dealing with a deep, unrelieved anger, bitterness, and hostility.

In this kind of uprising we see a classic illustration of activated hate. It is my interpretation, the reader may recall, that hate is a thick sludge of the heart. It is the slow accumulated distillation from bitterness, resentment, frustration, and hostility. It is not active. Something has to reconstitute it or recharge it into a churning, fermenting agent. As an ingredient in personality, it is scarcely in evidence even as an element in motivation. Something has to trigger it so that it becomes a powerful, often mindless, driving energy. Paradoxically, the nationwide daily discussion of civil rights by all media of communication, the unprecedented length of the Senate filibuster on the Civil Rights legislation, which despite its negative aspects gave important content to the public mind and the private understanding of the American people, and the final passage of the Bill itself—these were among the crucial elements that activated the residue of hate in Harlem, Rochester, Patterson, and Jersey City. Bitterness, hostility, and anger marked the reconverting of hate to the elements which created it. And now they had an outlet, a channel. The racial element as such was practically

83

coincidental. True, the form which the conflict took was defined by the starkest aspects of black-white struggle. But the important thing to be remembered is that as human beings who had been long since depersonalized, pickled, and preserved in and by hate, they were becoming aware of themselves as members of the human family—not as Negro members of the human family. In this awareness they became acutely sensitive to all the immediate forces in their environment that stood squarely in the way of their individual and collective self-realization. These forces were symbolized by the ever-present policeman who seemed always the guardian at the gate to hold them back, by the neighborhood merchant who was ever available to fatten himself on their poverty and hunger, and by some of their own "leaders" who championed causes, but who, they felt, did not speak for them.

In all of this nightmare of violence and rampage there is the basis for real hope. The hate is active, it is uncongealed, it is fluid, volatile, and dynamic hostility. This means that things that have been smoldering are now moving into the open and are thereby becoming available to be dealt with, shared, and treated. They are in reach of the resources of the community. A common agenda becomes available now for the first time, thus making communication possible. There must be brought to bear on the human issues that are now precipitated into focus all the wisdom, skill, and courage available within the area, the region and the nation. At whatever cost in dollars, facilities, and human creativity, the vast energies of hostilities and bitterness must be converted into hope, confidence, and hard rewarding effort which will destroy the nesting place of resentment and self-rejection.

Of course, none of this is to say that the rampage and destruction of life and property seems tolerable in any respect. Far from it. These outbursts must be contained and stopped! But to stop them under the police power of the state, which is the state's responsibility, must not obscure the other responsibilities of the state. This fact is becoming increasingly clear as evidenced by a wide variety of activity, planning, and implementation. The error must not be made that the state is dealing with Negroes; the state is dealing with *citizens*. There are no degrees in citizenship; a person cannot be almost a citizen but not quite. He is a citizen or he is not a citizen. The definition of a citizen is inherent, given under our form of government. It is not a prerogative that any group within the society has the right or the capability of conferring upon other individuals or groups within the society.

Out of the ferment may come a respect for law which has not hitherto been evident. The symbol of the cheap regard for law in these areas is the very existence of the long established ghetto with its bulwark of segregation. If this pattern is demolished, not as an act of good will or enlightenment merely, but because it is a violation of law, then a new respect for law will emerge. It must be remembered that law serves as a tutor. It provides a rallying point for the indecisive man as well as for the man who wishes to develop civic character. The lack of civic character is perhaps the most dramatic manifestation of the disrespect for law and order. T. R. Glover in interpreting the fall of the Roman Empire suggests that the empire collapsed because the average Roman citizen had lost his sense of responsibility for the life of the empire. In other words, he had civic privileges, but little civic responsibility. Without civic responsibility, there can be no civic character. At this point, the relevancy of respect for laws and order is inescapable.

85

Ghetto dwellers are not permitted to carry, and are often regarded as not being capable of carrying, civic responsibility; it is therefore hardly reasonable to expect them to have a real sense of civic character. The most often heard indictment of them is that they have no civic character while at the same time they are denied active civic responsibility without which there can be no civic character.

Before leaving the discussion on the attitude toward law, it is self-evident that in such a climate those who feel that the law is not for them but against them may find it easy to function with a sense of being outside the law. The attitude itself may not be one of lawlessness, but it most certainly breeds lawlessness. If a man is convinced that he is not regarded by law except when his behavior or his presence precipitates conflict with those who are favored by law, then the rest of his life that is lived out of contact with the favored ones is nominally beyond the consideration of the law. If this be the case, then it is possible for lawlessness to abound. This accounts for the fact that very often within the segregated community there is apt to be a blatant disregard for law and order. Again and again when some legal offense is perpetrated by a Negro against another Negro, the tendency of the law-enforcement authorities is to react with a bland indifference or a half-hearted urgency. After all, they are only Negroes and it is one Negro against another.

●

But there is still another dimension here. Under the pattern of segregation the Negro seems to be outside the law for the most part, while white persons tend to be beyond the law in their behavior toward Negroes. This is where the pattern is most effective; the favored ones can deal with the unfavored ones with legal irresponsibility. It is to be noted that this whole picture is undergoing change but the change is far from complete. Just within most recent months, covering the period from January 1, 1963, to the present, there have been individual and group murders, kidnapings, bombings, with very few arrests and as these lines are being written, not a single conviction and sentencing. It may seem that what is being commented on here is but a part of a larger national mood of legal irresponsibility. Be that is it may, the fact that will not be downed is that in the large picture, acts against the law are generally regarded as "acts against law and order," but in the area of the relations between black and white, such acts are not judged as being violations of law and order. They are special instances fitting into some kind of category of exception and therefore are not morally binding. They are not merely extralegal, but they are extramoral. And this is the radical difference. Law is not resisted; it is ignored.

In the matter of resistance to law, it must be taken into account that there are those in our society, both black and white, who resist the law in response to what they regard as a higher law.

For on that broad road of opposition to law and authority, along which stream the millions of humanity too low to grasp even the value of laws and institutions about them, resisting them from an ignorant and blind selfishness which makes them believe they are improving their own conditions by violating them, there are found walking men of a totally different order—white-robed sons of the gods with the light on their foreheads, who have left the narrow paths walled in by laws and conventions, not because they were too weak to walk in them, or because the goals towards which they led were too high, but because infinitely higher goals and straighter paths were calling to them—the new pathfinders of the race! These men, who rise as high above the laws and conventions of their social world as the mass who violate them fall below, are yet inextricably blended with them in the stream of souls who walk in the path of resistance to law. From the monk Telemachus, who, springing into the Roman arena to stop the gladiatorial conflict, fell, violating the laws and conventions of his society—a criminal, but almost a god—up and down all the ages man has been on earth there have been found these social resisters and violators of the accepted order, the saviors and leaders of men on the path to higher forms of life.*

Wherever such persons resist laws of segregation by trespassing, for instance, it is their idea that the law proscribing such trespassing is in itself amoral, if not immoral, and against the formal commitment of the society as expressed in the Constitution and the Bill of Rights. For the most part it is not a clear instance of resistance on moral grounds per se but on legal grounds which are in default by limiting statutes. It is therefore the existence of the limiting statutes that must be challenged by resistance. It is for this reason that the legal or constitutional grounds cannot be easily separated from the moral grounds. Thus the case for nonviolent resistance to the limiting statutes cannot ever seem to be clear of certain legal involvements. With reference to Gandhi, there was not the same kind of issue. He had a wide-open field to establish the grounds of his claim in the name of truth because there was no binding Bill of Rights or Constitution affecting the morality

* Olive Schreiner, *From Man to Man* (New York: Harper & Brothers, 1927), pp. 174-75.

of imperialism. The Indians were not Englishmen. India was property of the British government, but it was not England.

●

Despite all that has been said about the pattern of segregation in our society, it is my conviction that time is against it. In fact, much of the current effort to hold the line may be viewed as a back-against-the-wall endeavor. The more the world becomes a neighborhood in which time and space are approaching zero as a limit, the more urgent becomes the issue of neighborliness. Man can now circle the entire earth's surface in a matter of minutes. Communication is now instant! This means that the external symbols of segregation—the wall, the ghetto, the separate locale as a mandatory restriction binding upon groups of people because of race, color, creed, or national origin—cannot survive modern life. The emphasis here is upon the two words "external symbols." When I suggest that time is against the pattern of segregation, I am referring to the symbols. The walls are crumbling—this is one of the dramatic facts of our world. The fact itself is very frightening to many who have lived always behind the walls, within the walls, or beyond the walls. It is deeply disturbing also to those who have found the existence of the walls essential to their own peace, well-being, and security. Out of sight, out of mind—this can no longer be the case.

So much emphasis is placed upon the fact of the existence of the walls that the symbolic fact of the walls is ignored or is an unknown quantity. It must be remembered that segregation is a mood, a state of mind, and its external manifestation *is* external.

89

The root of the evil, and evil it is, is in the human spirit. Laws which make segregation illegal may or may not attack the root of the evil. Their great function is to deny the binding character of the external symbol by giving it no legal standing. They alert the body politic to the variety of external manifestations of the mood, the state of mind, and declare that wherever such manifestations appear, they are not to stand. This is most important because it calls attention to that of which segregation is the manifestation. As such it becomes a tutor or a guide for the human spirit. The law cannot deal with the human spirit directly. This is not within its universe of discourse.

What happens when the external symbol is outlawed and the walls of segregation are razed to the ground is a concern of the law only at the point that safeguards are being erected against other external symbols. And this is of vast importance—though negative basically. The reaction of the human spirit that has lived under the pattern of segregation on both sides of the wall, when the wall is removed, is apt to be one of panic and profound mental and spiritual distress. When my family and I lived on the campus of Howard University, our front yard was enclosed by a picket fence along the outside of which was a sidewalk leading from the main walk of the campus to the street. We had a dog whose name was Beariemore. It was his chief-in-the-yard sport to lie upon the steps facing the direction of the main walk, watching for the appearance of a Western Union boy coming toward the fence on his bicycle. Beariemore would wait for him at the corner of the fence, bark him all the way, the full length of the yard, and send him on his way. Then he would return to his former waiting position. One day after a very heavy snowfall, there were snowdrifts four to five feet high in one corner of the yard. Beariemore began his game

90

as usual. Only this time when he chased one of the boys he did not take the snowdrift into account. I heard him yelp as if he were in great pain. I ran to the door, thinking that someone had hurt him. He was all right except that when he found himself over the fence with no barrier between him and the Western Union boy, he panicked. People who are conditioned to living behind the walls and those whose emotional security is dependent upon the stability of the walls are apt to be seized by a sense of panic, not only if the walls are removed, but if their removal is imminent. Such a condition is spiritual.

At such a time the real task of making or building a decent society of equality will emerge. Since segregation is the manifestation of a state of mind and mood of the human spirit, in a situation of threat a new and more subtle manifestation of the mood may appear. The wall is in the mind and in the spirit.

The situation is apt to be aggravated by the fact that the wall has existed so long that it may no longer be regarded as a symbol but as the thing itself. Wherever this is the case, the removal of the wall is thought to be the riddance of segregation. When I was a college boy in Atlanta, our football team played a team of regular army men from a Negro regiment. At dinner in the evening before the game, the behavior of the soldiers was very crude and somewhat embarrassing. At the next chapel service, the dean of the college, in commenting on the behavior of the soldiers, said, "It is a long way from slavery to a sense of freedom and no former slave or former slave owner can make it in fifty years."

The issue then is twofold. The walls that divide must be demolished. They must be cast down, destroyed, uprooted. This is beyond debate. There must be ceaseless and unrelenting pressure to that end, using all the resources of our common life. These

91

barriers must be seen for what they are, a disease of our society, the enemy of human decency and humane respect. In many ways, they are so much a part of our landscape that they seem to belong to the landscape and as such are regarded as germane to the American way of life. The resistance against their reversal is so rooted that it has created a new term in the current vocabulary—backlash. As has been suggested earlier, the walls seem so permanent that to advocate their removal must be conditional: those who are the obvious sufferers because of their presence must prove themselves worthy of such action. In other words, the walls are sacrosanct and to tamper with them can be done only out of a mood of grace and compassion. In fine, the walls have an established right to be, even though what this right is, is never quite clear and he who would remove the walls must show cause. Their destruction is such a monumental undertaking and is calling for such huge costs in human lives, resources of money, time, and energy, that an ever-widening weariness is apt to sweep over the land in the wake of the crumbling of the walls. And this is the danger. When the walls are down, it is then that the real work of building the healthy American society begins. The razing of the walls is prelude—important, critical, urgent, vital, but prelude nevertheless. About this there must be no mistake.

●

The removal of the walls is the first step in the attack on the mood of which they are a manifestation. Care must be exercised to see to it that new walls will not be built. One of the things that will make it easier to build new walls of segregation in the form of new kinds of discrimination is what has been aptly called the discrimination gap which is the huge burden of the American Negro. This aspect of the issue has been effectively described by Whitney Young, the Executive Director of the National Urban League, in his recent book *To Be Equal*: "For at this moment in history, if the United States honestly drops legal, practical, and subtle racial barriers to employment, housing, education, public accommodations, health and welfare facilities and services, the American Negro still will not achieve full equality in our lifetime." He goes on to say that "more than three centuries of abuse, humiliation, segregation, and bias have burdened the Negro with a handicap that will not automatically slip from his shoulders as discriminatory laws and practices are abandoned. The situation is much like that of two men running the mile in a track meet. One is well-equipped, wears track shoes and runs on cinders. The other is barefoot and runs in sand. Seeing that one runner is outdistancing the other with ease, you then put track shoes on the second fellow and place him on the cinder track also. Seconds later it should surprise no one to see that the second runner is still yards behind and will never catch up unless something else is done to even the contest."*

All the damage done by the existence of the walls must be repaired and healed. It is not a part of the work of this essay to suggest such a program. I know of no more comprehensive, clear, and creative blueprint to this end than is set forth in Whitney Young's book.

The other aspect of the issue has to do with the mood, the state of mind out of which discrimination and the response to dis-

* New York: McGraw-Hill Book Company, 1964, pp. 22-23.

crimination come in the first instance. The issue is a moral and spiritual one and falls within the broad and specific scope of morality and religion. The point of departure for this final aspect of my discussion is to be found at the beginning of the essay where reference is made to the fact that Negroes and white persons are often excluded from each other's magnetic field of value. The first step in giving the kind of new orientation that will bring one into moral focus is the loss of fear. When the relationship between the groups is devoid of fear, then it becomes possible for them to relate to each other as human beings and have far more that unites them than divides them.

The burden of being black and the burden of being white is so heavy that it is rare in our society to experience oneself as a human being. It may be, I do not know, that to experience oneself as a human being is one with experiencing one's fellows as human beings. Precisely what does it mean to experience oneself as a human being? In the first place, it means that the individual must have a sense of kinship to life that transcends and goes beyond the immediate kinship of family or the organic kinship that binds him ethnically or "racially" or nationally. He has to feel that he belongs to his total environment. He has a sense of being an essential part of the structural relationship that exists between him and all other men, and between him, all other men, and the total external environment. As a human being, then, he belongs to life and the whole kingdom of life that includes all that lives and perhaps, also, all that has ever lived. In other words, he sees himself as a part of a continuing, breathing, living existence. To be a human being, then, is to be essentially alive in a living world.

I like to feel that strange life beating up against me. I like to realize forms of life utterly unlike mine. When my own life feels small, and I am oppressed with it, I like to crush together, and see it in a picture, in an instant, a multitude of disconnected unlike phases of human life—a mediaeval monk with his string of beads pacing the quiet orchard, and looking up from the grass at his feet to the heavy fruit trees; little Malay boys playing naked on a shining sea-beach; a Hindu philosopher alone under his banyan tree, thinking, thinking, thinking, so that in the thought of God he may lose himself; a troop of Bacchanalians dressed in white, with crowns of vine-leaves, dancing along the Roman streets; a martyr on the night of his death looking through the narrow window to the sky, and feeling that already he has the wings that shall bear him up; an epicurean discoursing at a Roman bath to a knot of his disciples on the nature of happiness; a Kaffir witch-doctor, seeking for herbs by moonlight, while from the huts on the hill-side come the sound of dogs barking, and the voices of women and children; a mother giving bread and milk to her children in little wooden basins and singing the evening song. I like to see it all: I feel it run through me—that life belongs to me; it makes my little life larger; it breaks down the narrow walls that shut me in.*

In a conversation with three Indian chiefs in one of the Canadian provinces, I was deeply impressed particularly by the reply of one of them to the query, "Are you a Canadian and then an Indian, or are you an Indian and then a Canadian?" His reply, as it came through the interpreter, was essentially this: "I come from some miles near the Arctic circle in the north country. I live with the snow, the ice, the sharp wind in the winter; with the streams, the flowing waters, the sun and the blossoms in summer. These flow into me and I flow into them. They keep me and I keep them. I am a part of them and they are a part of me. I am not sure what you mean when you say Indian or Canadian."

* Olive Schreiner, *The Story of an African Farm* (London: Ernest Benn, Ltd., 1951 ed.), pp. 201-2.

What he is saying is that he has a sense of being a part of an extended life that belongs to him and to which he belongs. Instead of its spreading him out so that all the margins of the self fade and vanish away, it deepens and intensifies his essential sense of uniqueness without the devastation of a sense of being different. The same basic principle was manifested by an experience in Nigeria. At the close of a lecture before the Press Club, to which reference has been made, I was invited to a small room for refreshments. I asked for a kind of soft drink called ginger beer. My host opened the bottle, poured a little on the floor as he said, "For my ancestors," and then he filled my glass. In this concept of the extended family, as I saw it, there is a variation of the same theme. To experience oneself as a human being is to know a sense of kinship with one's total environment and to recognize that it is this structural relationship that makes it possible for one to experience himself as a human *being*. Being white or black becomes merely incidental and is of no basic significance. Does this seem far-fetched and speculative or unrealistic?

What is meant here can be most clearly understood if we look at the conditions that obtain when differences of race, culture, ethnic, or national origin are sloughed off, when the essential fact of being a human being in the world is brought sharply into focus. In times of disaster, when the only thing that is relevant is that a man is stripped of all superficial categories that separate and divide, one gets some notion of what it means just to be a human being in the world among other human beings who are all structurally bound together by a total environment. Flood, earthquakes, disaster, know nothing of race or class. "God causes his sun to shine on the just and the unjust, his rain to fall on the evil and the good."

96

In our own country, when the national life is threatened, we make common cause in which for the moment everybody is counted in as an essential human being, possessed of certain resources that are needful for the survival of the common life. Despite the fact that this is an act of desperation and convenience, which act may be so interpreted by all, nevertheless the salutary effect obtains in the lives of those who are counted *in* merely because they are needed. As ironical as this is, nevertheless, the national registration during the last World War made an important impact on the life of Negroes, particularly in the South. A man who had been called "J.B." all his life and who knew no other name had to make a name for himself out of the initials. Think of what it meant to this man who had been regarded by his society as without name or significance to find himself suddenly on the receiving end of personal attention from the vast federal government. Now his name was known, his address duly noted, and his *intention* to be a consumer of certain goods such as meat, sugar, gasoline, and automobile tires was registered. An entirely fresh dimension of personal awareness opened out before him. He began to experience himself as a human being. The fact that the new status was crisis-created must not obscure what was really at work here. The new experience did not know anything about a crisis situation.

●

But it is not only the situation of collective crisis that creates a climate in which the individual human being emerges with an experience of himself as a human being. Here at last we come face to face with the original claim of religion and here I refer

97

especially to the ethical insight brought into the stream of contemporary life by the Judaeo-Christian tradition.

It is most unfortunate that the trustees of this insight, namely the religious institutions, have failed singularly to witness to the insight. The impact upon the individual when he experiences himself as a human being is to regard himself as being of infinite worth. Such a sense of worth is not confined by narrow limits of the self so that worth may be determined by contrast with something or someone of less worth. No, this is a specious basis for ascertaining worth. Such a sense of worth is rooted in one's own consciousness which expands and expands until there is involved the totality of life itself. As important as is the clue to one's self-estimate, as found in the attitude of others in the environment, this is not now what is at issue. To experience oneself as a human being is to feel life moving through one and claiming one as a part of it. It is like the moment of insight into a new idea or an aspect of truth. What initially is grasped by the mind and held there for meaning begins slowly or suddenly to *hold* the mind as if the mind itself is being thought by a vaster and greater Mind. It is like the thing that happens when you are trying to explain something to a child and you finally succeed in doing so. Then the child says, "I see." In that moment you are no longer there in fact. The barrier that stood between the child's comprehension of the idea and the idea itself has been removed. There is a flowing together, as if the child and the idea were alone in all the universe!

The ultimate meaning of experience is felt in such a way that all of oneself is included. It is total, it is unified and unifying. It is not the experience of oneself as male or female, as black or

98

white, as American or European. It is rather the experience of oneself as *being*. It is at such a time that one can hear the sound of the genuine in other human beings. This is to be able to identify with them. One man's response to the sound of the genuine in another man is to ascribe to the other man the same sense of infinite worth that one holds for oneself. When this happens, men are free to relate to each other as human beings—good, bad, mean, friendly, prejudiced, altruistic, but human beings. Whatever may be the nature of the shortcomings, they are seen from the view on the other side where the person lives whose shortcomings are being encountered.

This is the precious work of the imagination. There is an apt quotation in Russell Gordon Smith's *Fugitive Papers*: "On the seventh day, therefore, God could not rest. In the morning and the evening He busied Himself with terrible and beautiful concoctions and in the twilight of the seventh day He finished that which is of more import than the beasts of the earth and the fish of the sea and the lights of the firmament. And he called it Imagination because it was made in His own image; and those unto whom it is given shall see God."*

The place where the imagination shows its greatest power as the agent of God is in the miracle which it creates when one man, standing where he is, is able, while remaining there, to put himself in another man's place. Many years ago I was the overnight guest in the house of a friend. I was seated the next morning in the living room reading the morning paper. His little boy rode into the room in his kiddy car, stopped it in front of me, and said, "Mr. Thurman, will you please help me change my tire, I just had

* New York: Columbia University Press, 1930, p. 96.

a blowout." I helped him jack up his car, take the old tire off, replace it with a spare, and then remove the jack. He sat in his car, stepped on the starter, but the motor would not start. He pulled out the choke; nothing happened. He got out of the car, opened each side of the hood, tinkered a little, then tried again with the same results. Then a strange thing happened. His shoulders became very stiff, a grim look swept over his tender countenance, and words flowed forth from his lips that were taken verbatim from his father under such circumstances. Still nothing happened. He got out of the car and came around to me. "Mr. Thurman, lend me your pencil." With my pencil in hand, he opened the gas tank of his car, put the pencil down into it, held it up to the light. "Ah, the tank is empty. No wonder it wouldn't start." He rushed out to the kitchen, came back with a glass of water, sat in his kiddy car, drank the water, started the motor, and rode out of the living room, through the dining room and into the kitchen.

This is the idea. A man can send his imagination forth to establish a beachhead in another man's spirit, and from that vantage point so to blend with the other's landscape that what he sees and feels is authentic—this is the great adventure in human relations. But this is not enough. The imagination must report its findings accurately without regard to prejudgments and private or collective fears. But this too is not enough. There must be both a spontaneous and a calculating response to such knowledge which will result in sharing of life and resources at their deepest level.

This is to experience onself as a human being and to have that essential experience illumined and underscored by experiencing one's fellows as human beings. This is what every persons seeks to have happen to himself. Every man lives under the necessity for being at home in his own house, as it were. He must not seem to himself to be alien to himself. This is the thing that happens when other human beings relate to him as if he were not a human being or less than a human being. It is possible for a man to declassify whole groups of people on the basis of certain criteria which he establishes or which he inherits. For instance, it may be to denigrate all people who come from a particular country, locale, or region, or all who speak a certain language, or all whose skin has pigmentation of any kind or a particular kind, or all who claim a different religious faith.

It may be that the experience of which we speak is not possible unless and until the individual sees himself as being contained or held by something so much more than he is that his life is brought into a focus of self-conscious meaning and value. Such an experience is possible only in the light of ultimate values and ultimate meanings. And this is what religion undertakes to guarantee; the extent to which Christianity is religious is the extent to which it would guarantee such an experience for the individual.

Once when I was very young, my grandmother, sensing the meaning of the constant threat under which I was living, told me about the message of one of the slave ministers on her plantation. Whatever he developed as his theme on the rare occasions when he was able to hold services for his fellow slaves, the climactic moment came in these exhilarating words: "You are not slaves; you are not *niggers* condemned forever to do your master's will— you are God's children." When those words were uttered a warm glow crept all through the very being of the slaves, and they felt the feeling of themselves run through them. Even at this far distance I can relive the pulsing tremor of raw energy that was released in me as I responded to her words. The sense of being permanently grounded in God gave to the people of that far-off time a way to experience themselves as human beings.

But this is one side of the coin. The community of believers must be involved in the same kind of experience. The normal reaction to experiencing oneself as a human being is to seek to experience other people as human beings. This does not have to be in the name of religion exclusively. Such a reaction is automatic unless there is some kind of intervention which short-circuits the process. The thing that determines the character of how one relates to one's fellows in any manner that has personal meaning in it, is shaped by how the individual defines others. This is but another aspect of the issue as discussed earlier. The community of Christian believers are under the judgment of a command to love God, which is the response to the awareness that God cares or loves the individual and one must love one's neighbor as oneself.

●

There has emerged in the tradition of the Christian movement a secondary consideration, which is that the Christian must love especially those who are Christians. Here is a tie that binds all Christians as members of the Body of Christ. If this is the case, then to be a part of the Body of Christ is to share the love of all those who are a part of the Body of Christ. To spell it out: not only would a Baptist be under the demand to love all other Baptists and a Methodist to love all other Methodists, etc., but it would be binding upon each one who claimed to be a Christian, and therefore a part of the Body of Christ, to love all others who make such a claim. It would follow then that the Christian would be unique among other men in that the Christian is secure in the love of other Christians. Indeed at one time in the history of Christianity it was this that separated the Christian from the world. "Behold how the Christians love each other." The formula can be stated categorically: the Christian has a special sense of being loved by God because he accepts the idea that God loved him by giving His son for his redemption. His response to the redemptive giving of God is to love God. "I love him because he first loved me." All Christians are involved in this relationship with God, therefore all Christians must give love to one another as a part of the giving of love to God.

The tragedy is that even among those whose profession of faith subscribes completely to the above, the total relationship gives evidence of another kind. In fact, it is precisely accurate to say that the church, which is the institutional expression of the doctrine, has given little indication that being a member of the Body of Christ has any bearing on how one member relates to the other members. Granted it may be less evident among those who are a part of the same sectarian tradition. There is much to indicate that the further a particular group may be from the so-called mainstream of the convention of the doctrine, the more apt we may be to find the practice of love of all who belong to the household of faith. One of my earliest memories is of greeting people at our door who asked for my parents because they wanted to talk to them about religion. Two things I remember: they called themselves Russellites, and despite the fact that they were white they made themselves at home in the living room. Nothing entered into what they did or what they said that drew the color line.

Until most recently, no one expected the white Christian to

love the black Christian or the black Christian to love the white Christian. Historically in this country, the church has given the sweep of its moral force to the practice of segregation within its own community of believers. To the extent to which this has been done, the church has violated one of the central elements in its own commitment. It has dared to demonstrate that the commitment is not central, that it does not believe that Christians are bound to love one another.

The effect of its position with reference to Christians of other races is far-reaching. It is to be noted that the doctrine has to be accommodated and dealt with in a manner that will hold the doctrine secure and at the same time tolerate its profound violation. How is this accomplished? With reference to the Negro, the church has promulgated a doctrine that makes the Negro the object of its salvation while at the same time it denies him the status of a human being, thereby enhancing the difficulties he must face in his effort to experience himself as a human being. Time after weary time, the church has dishonored its Lord. When I asked Mr. Ganhdi, "What is the greatest handicap that Jesus has in India?" instantly he replied, "Christianity." And this is what he meant.

The purpose here is not to indict but rather it is to lament the fact that such is the situation. The point must be clear that the commitment to love as it stands at the center of the Christian doctrine of God has not prevented the Christian from excluding Negroes from his Christian fellowship, nor has it prevented the Christian who is Negro from excluding white people from his Christian fellowship. To the extent that this is true, being Christian may not involve a person either in experiencing himself as

104

a human being or in relating to others so as to experience them as human beings. The sad fact is that being Jewish, Catholic, or Protestant seems to make little difference in this regard.

If being Christian does not demand that all Christians love each other and thereby become deeply engaged in experiencing themselves as human beings, it would seem futile to expect that Christians as Christians would be concerned about the secular community in its gross practices of prejudice and discrimination. If a black Christian and a white Christian, in encounter, cannot reach out to each other in mutual realization because of that which they are experiencing in common, then there should be no surprise that the Christian institution has been powerless in the presence of the color bar in society. Rather it has reflected the presence of the color bar within its own institutional life.

On the other hand, if Christians practiced brotherhood among Christians, this would be one limited step in the direction of a new order among men. Think of what this would mean. Wherever one Christian met or dealt with another Christian, there would be a socially redemptive encounter. They would be like the Gulf Stream or the Japanese Current tempering and softening the climate in all directions. Indeed the Christian would be a leaven at all levels of the community and in public and private living. Of course, such a situation may lend itself to all kinds of exploitation and betrayals— but the Christian would be one of the bulwarks of integrity in human relations in an immoral society.

If the Christian limited his practice to other Christians, thereby guaranteeing that the church, wherever it existed, at whatever cost, would not tolerate segregation within its body, then there would be a kind of fierce logic in its position. It would be consistent within itself because it would practice brotherhood without regard to race, color, and all the other barriers. It would make for a kind of arrogance and bigotry toward those who were not fortunate or wise enough to put themselves in the way of being Christian. This would narrow the basis of the faith deliberately, while at the same time providing enough room for the outsider to come in and belong. But the church has historically tended to reject this alternative.

It is true and freely acknowledged that there are many changes afoot. Here and there through the years the Gospel has been at work despite the prohibition placed upon it by many denials. There is a power in the teaching which, when released, goes on to work its perfect work. Slowly there have emerged certain ingredients in the social climate that have had a softening effect. Much of this is due to the introduction of the teachings of Jesus and the Christian religious experience into society.

In recent time it has become increasingly a part of the public policy and private practice of the church to put itself squarely on the side of cleaning its own house of the evils that separate the brethren. It has become more and more aggressive in attacking the presence of those same evils wherever they are in our society. It is a prestige factor in the church to take a challenging position in the matter of the treatment of Negroes. Very often when I am visiting in a city, clergymen and laymen proudly announce that their particular church is "integrated," or they may complain that they are wide open in the welcome of Negroes but that Negroes do not come. One is glad to witness the changes that are taking place and may regard the changes as delayed reactions to the impact of the Gospel in the church itself. But the thought persists that this is the response of the church to the pressure of the secular community upon it, rather than the response of the church to the genius of the Gospel which it proclaims. Perhaps it is both. Even the church cannot be in the position of establishing the ground rules by which God works in the development of the good life for His children.

●

But why has the church been such a tragic witness to its own Gospel? It does seem to me at times that it is because the church is not sufficiently religious. By this I mean that it is not wide open to the Spirit of the living God. Its genius as an institution has to be sectarian in character. Perhaps there can be no such thing among men as the Church of God; it is the nature of institutionalism to be adjectival; some qualifying word must always precede the word "church." It has to be some *kind* of church, and this gives it its unique character and position.

This fact creates a terrible dilemma. How important is the limiting and defining character? It may be that the church as such is an abstraction which only becomes concrete when a peculiar pattern or style of worship, etiquette, or doctrine emerges to define the character and give context to the abstraction. Nothing is ultimately admissible that may threaten the institutional structure that gives to the Christian religion its form and substance. But suppose as a part of the form and substance of the church all believers must commit themselves to loving all men, believers and nonbelievers, as children of God and therefore members one of another? Then the tremendous resources of such a church would be at the disposal of the performing ethic. Under such a circumstance, the whole missionary-conversion process would be reversed—men would knock at the door of the church to find out what they need to do to become what, in evidence, the Christian is. The life that the church lives in the world would "bring the world to Christ." This surely means first of all to go ye into one's very own world, one's very own life, to go into every part of one's very own being and proclaim the good news that one can be free to experience oneself as a child of God and to experience all other men as children of God. Of such is a part of the miracle of Jesus. Men came to him with the searching question, What must I do? How may I? He made the life of God contagious!

The problem may not be so simple. It is too easy to say or to believe that the church has not been true to its own Gospel. The question that deserves probing is Why? Is it because of human frailty? Is it because man has not evolved to the point that he is sufficiently human to deal justly and to promote the common good? Is there some inherent limitation in the nature of man that works against his doing for himself and with and on behalf of others that which makes for harmony, wholeness, love? Is it because of what the church recognizes as original sin? If not, precisely from what is the believer saved by the death and resurrection of Christ? Are the roots of conflict deep into a long forgotten past?

Why is it that in many aspects of life that are regarded as secular one is apt to see more sharing, more of a tendency for human beings to experience themselves as human beings, than in those areas that are recognized as being religious? There seems to be more of a striving toward equality of treatment in many so-called secular institutions in our society than has characterized those institutions whose formal religious commitment demands that they practice the art of brotherhood. When I was in college, I heard

108

two Negro men arguing on this very issue. We were on an all-day train ride in the third of the day coach designated for Negroes. Finally, one of the men, to clinch his point, said, "If I had committed a crime and was being tried in court, I would much rather have a jury made up of gamblers, race track men, pimps, than one made up of people who profess Christianity. I know I'd get much fairer treatment."

There is something out of line somewhere. Can it be that matters which have to do with human relations are not the legitimate concern of religion? Hardly. The fact cannot be ignored that generally our society does not expect the church to be any kind of guide in these matters. It seems to me that one of the really tremendous things that is happening before our very eyes is that the religious community is now being judged by the same standards of human relations as the secular institutions in our society. This means that the church is slowly winning the right to be regarded as an institution that has a stake in the earthly fate of mankind. It has always concerned itself with charity, with good works, with the meeting of the creature needs of man; it has always concerned itself with the preaching of a doctrine of salvation which addressed itself to the spiritual condition as far as the soul was concerned; but for some reason that has puzzled me all of my life, the religious community tended not to concern itself with the total needs of a man as a human being. And that, after all, is what matters most. Always it is a human being who hungers, who is sick, who is ignorant, who suffers. And he cannot be touched in any way that counts unless the word gets through to him that he is being experienced as a human being by the persons for whom he is the object of good works.

Perhaps there is something inherent in the religious experience that always pulls back toward the personal center out of which the individual operates and the religious context that gives existential meaning to the experience itself. It is this latter frame of reference that creates the categories out of which the dogma of a particular faith comes. In this sense it may seem an unrealistic demand that religious experience be universal. If this is a true picture, then such notions or concepts as brotherhood, reverence for life, respect for personality, do not rightfully belong to the behavior pattern of the religious devotee. Such ideas would then invade the religious man's life from the wider context of his living, the areas of his life that are beyond and outside of the parochial and the sectarian character of his religious faith. I have often pondered the fact that men of different faiths may share common experiences which are outside of their specifically religious fellowship, and that on behalf of such demands they may make tremendous sacrifices, without feeling under any necessity to share the intimacy of their experience of God.

Or it may be in order to raise a question about the universality of an ethic which grows out of a sectarian or parochial religious experience. Could it be that we are face to face with an inherent weakness in religious experience, as such, that it is private, personal, and binding upon the individual only to the extent that he identifies himself with another and thereby becoming one with him at all the levels and all the ways that are significant? Here may be a clue, for wherever the Christian religious experience has made a difference in the one-to-one relationship of the believer, one sees this kind of private, personal identification at work. When I identify with a man, I become one with him and in him I see myself. I remember a quotation out of the past—the statement "know thyself" has been taken more mystically from the statement "thou hast seen thy brother, thou hast seen thy God." This is the true meaning of the reference earlier about listening for the sound of the genuine in another. Such an experience cannot become a dogma—it has to remain experiential all the way. It is a probing process trying to find the opening into another. And it requires exposure, sustained exposure. One of the great obstacles to such exposure is the fact of segregation.

The religious experience as I have known it seems to swing wide the door, not merely into Life but into lives. I am confident that my own call to the religious vocation cannot be separated from the slowly emerging disclosure that my religious experience makes it possible for me to experience myself as a human being and thus keep a very real psychological distance between myself and the hostilities of my environment. Through the years it has driven me more and more to seek to make as a normal part of my relations with men the experiencing of them as human beings. When this happens love has essential materials with which to work. And contrary to the general religious teaching, men would not need to stretch themselves out of shape in order to love. On the contrary, a man comes into possession of himself more completely when he is *free* to love another.

●

I have dwelt at length upon the necessity that is laid upon the church and the Christian because the Christian Church is still one of the major centers of influence in the American community. Too, the

111

Christian Church claims to be under the judgment of God as it fulfills itself in human history. But it must be remembered that what is true in any religion is to be found in that religion because it is true, it is not true because it is found in that religion. The ethical insight which makes for the most healthy and creative human relations is not the unique possession of any religion, however inspired it may be. It does not belong exclusively to any people or to any age. It has an ancient history, and it has been at work informing the quality of life and human relations longer than the records and the memories of man. Just as scattered through the earliest accounts of man's journey on this planet are flashes and shafts of light illuminating the meaning of man and his fellows, so in our times we find the widest variety of experiments pointing in the same direction and making manifest the same goals. Men are made for one another. In this grand discovery there is a disclosure of another dimension: this experience of one another is not enough. There is a meaning in life greater than, but informing, all the immediate meanings—and the name given to this meaning is religion, because it embodies, however faintly, a sense of the ultimate and the divine.

There is a spirit abroad in life of which the Judaeo-Christian ethic is but one expression. It is a spirit that makes for wholeness and for community; it finds its way into the quiet solitude of a Supreme Court justice when he ponders the constitutionality of an act of Congress which guarantees civil rights to all its citizens; it settles in the pools of light in the face of a little girl as with her frailty she challenges the hard frightened heart of a police chief; it walks along the lonely road with the solitary protest marcher and settles over him with a benediction as he falls by the assassin's bullet fired from ambush; it kindles the fires of unity in the heart of Jewish Rabbi, Catholic Priest, and Protestant Minister as they join arms together, giving witness to their God on behalf of a brotherhood that transcends creed, race, sex, and religion; it makes a path to Walden Pond and ignites the flame of nonviolence in the mind of a Thoreau and burns through his liquid words from the Atlantic to the Pacific; it broods over the demonstrators for justice and brings comfort to the desolate and forgotten who have no memory of what it is to feel the rhythm of belonging to the race of men; it knows no country and its allies are to be found wherever the heart is kind and the collective will and the private endeavor seek to make justice where injustice abounds, to make peace where chaos is rampant, and to make the voice heard on behalf of the helpless and the weak. It is the voice of God and the voice of man; it is the meaning of all the strivings of the whole human race toward a world of friendly men underneath a friendly sky.